THE WORLD TEACHER DISCLOSED

SIGNS AND EVIDENCES THAT HE'S AMONG US

A FIELD INVESTIGATION THAT PROVES GRIGORI GRABOVOI TO BE THE SECOND COMING OF JESUS CHRIST ON EARTH

BY YELENA LOGINOVA

INTRODUCTION

There cannot be a prudent Messianism that can take care of earthly affairs well. Based on its mystical nature, Messiah is the victim, nd the Nation - Messiah can be sacrificed by them.

(N. Berdyaev)

This book is based on my research, which is essentially a large gathering of evidence, ranging from prophecies (both ancient and new), recent declarations from high-level people around the world, as well as some statements in the words of the World Teacher himself and my own personal experiences, tending to proovve that the Second Coming of Christ in visible form has occurred, that he was born in a conventional, natural and easy way. All elements in this book follow a logical sequence, coming together to form a perfect puzzle, and each aspect can be further broadened and deepened almost to infinity.

I therefore set some limits to the scope of this present work, but did my best for it still to be utterly fascinating and to stir awakening in your mind and heart.

Of course, if you do not agree with me, I can understand your doubts. However, it should be noted that no one has yet managed to move my ideas from the position where I stand firmly and joyously, but do not think for a minute that my conclusions are based in fanaticism, far from it, actually.

I'm at my core a genuinely free individual, of a very inquisitive nature. I try to look at the world in its totality and to move toward the goal which is Eternal and Harmonious Development for all.

Jesus promised his disciples to return, but did not indicate the exact date or place, so it is always awaiting us. It would be very interesting to create an encyclopedia of false Christs in the past two millennia, of all those who proclaimed themselves as the Savior and to classify them, to consider in more detail the nature and characteristics of their psyche and, more importantly, of their knowledge and plan for bringing peace on Earth.

I think that the results would be quite amusing, touching, and in some cases, quite saddening.

Yet in the Bible we have a hint of time. Jesus in his conversation with his students once remarked that he would return after two days, but it was left at that without being understood. However, in the same Bible, Jesus Christ once accidentally said that one day of our Father - is a thousand years.

So, would have he been talking about today's historical period?

I think that no one would dispute the fact that the human consciousness has rapidly reached an accelerated pace on the planet in the last hundred years.

There are Helena Petrovna Blavatsky, Helena Roerich, and Alice Bailey, from England. I am sure that you have heard of these famous messengers of Truth. Yet we can find very specific information about the imminent Coming of the World Teacher highlighted in the book "A NEW PHENOMENON OF CHRIST" by *Alice Bailey*.

For 30 years she has telepathically received information transmitted to her by Djwhal Khul - lama of all lamas directly cooperating with the Masters of the legendary Shambhala.

I think that some people, reading these lines, could be grinning. This is - your right, but still would recommend you not to draw too prematured conclusions on the matter.

Christianity forbids channeling, calling this kind of information sinful pastime, to say the least. All messages from various entities and mentors, conveyed to "channels" (contactees), are automatically considered by orthodox Christians as demonic manifestations. However, if you're not in such a hurry to put labels on the subject, it would appear that the way had been shown by very well-known historical figures and some religious books, which could be classified as channeling. Judge for yourself. Here is a quote from the book "God's law for families and schools," which was published in 1987, by the Russian Orthodox Church: "Divine revelation can be seen in all the things through which God has revealed Himself and in the exercise of the true faith in Him. God lets Himself known through special people, unusual ways, or as we say, supernatural occurrences- this is when God reveals Himself directly or through the angels."

Since not all people are able to receive revelation directly from God. Then God chooses special, righteous people who can be granted this revelation. The first were the messengers who spoke the word of God: Adam, Noah, Moses and other prophets and righteous people."

Among the Apostles of the New Testament that could be presented as "channel", let's refer to St. John the Evangelist, who wrote one of the Gospels and the Apocalypse. Among the Orthodox icons, we can find a character called "John the Evangelist in silence." On John's left shoulder is shown an angel of the Holy Spirit who whispers into the ear of the evangelist his message.

Nonetheless, Christian churches, as we already noted, did not support channeling. Those suspected of "Fellowship with devils" in the Middle Ages simply could be burned at a stake, even if they themselves claimed to be communicating with the angels or saints.

CHAPTER 1

Jeane, I found him!

"Some information about the author of this study".

*"To see a world in a grain of sand
And heaven in a wild flower,
Hold infinity in the palm of your hand
And eternity in an hour."*

"William Blake"

    I quite consciously state, not only based on a direct inner knowing, but also after having done tremendous research prooving it, that Grigori Grabovoi is a long-awaited Messiah, the World Teacher, or the Second Coming of Christ which manifested on Earth in 1963, as a person, as a normal earthly man, born in Kazakhstan.

No one tried to convince me - I just know for sure in my soul and attempted to prove this fact logically to myself, which resulted here in this particular research. You may ask yourself, why should you trust such information, coming from me? Are not there already self-declared Messiahs, as well as many false Christs in the past two millennia?

What makes Grigori Grabovoi different from those who confidently proclaimed themselves as the Savior but that History could not confirm? Of course, this is a reasonable question.

    I can feel your ironic smile. I can read your thoughts, more or less as follows: "Well, another crazy fanatic, who got under the spell of this strange psychic.

Most likely, she had some serious drama in her life, and this lady just found another comfort, believing the promises and utopian ideas of the impostor." In general, women tend to be bizarre and hysterical and not very capable of reasoning. In short, it is as old as the hills and even boring. I understand you, and, of course, in some cases, that's how it happens, but not with me, forgive me for my immodesty. I'll try to be, as much as I can, honest, and you make your conclusions.

I want to assure you that I did not have any life drama that pushed me in that direction. Yes, like for most people, I've been faced with all sorts of collisions, and there were sometimes very difficult situations, even critical ones. But despite this, I consider myself as a happy person and my life is truly filled with love, diversity, creativity, and that raises such a spontaneous feeling of joy in my soul.

I must confess that even through the tragic events I strive to look at them from the standpoint of an observer, and make the choice to communicate only with those I want to, cutting off from harmful relationships.

I must say that, from observing myself with an interesting perspective on personal reactions to events and people I never expected , which manifested themselves in any given situation.

In this life, I have two diplomas: mechanical engineer and chemical engineering. That sounds modest, but my job over there was very specific: At the university in Russia where I went to, I studied technology of explosives, and began working in a closed Engineering Design Center. It is no longer a military secret, as the plant I used to work in, no longer exists, and the form of access to the secrets has already expired...

Then the members of my family and I had to unexpectedly and rapidly immigrate to the U.S. What has happened with virtually no effort on our part, I had a lot of interviews for work but never felt quite satisfied with any of what I found, went to Boston for medical college and become a nurse. Which I miraculously managed to complete, becoming a nurse, which to my utmost surprise, is a very prestigious profession in this country.

My work in medicine took away my rose-colored glasses and dispelled any and all illusions about the subtle human nature.

I was faced with the unpleasant and somewhat scary sides of today's human reality. I was born in Russia, in Siberia. My dad was the boss of a large organization and a Communist. He had a personal driver, and my beautiful mom walked in high heels and her nails were always long and painted. I grew up a happy, spoiled, and curious child whose freedom was never limited. I remember at age nine I went to the library and read a scientific article for teenagers about the structure of atoms, among other topics. I wanted to understand how this world worked.

On my own initiative, when I was 15 years old, I began to study complex mathematics course at the University of Novosibirsk at Academic city, and felt pleasure at solving difficult and unusual mathematical problems.

My parents were very happy and healthy, and were quite far away from any religion. The concept of God was very abstract and far-fetched for them and therefore for me as well.

But one winter when I was 12 years old, I looked up and saw the night sky full of stars. Suddenly I was attracted by a small constellation of seven stars and one of them suddenly caused in my soul a strange joy. I looked at this star and unexpectedly in my head; I heard a very clear voice. It was not my thought.

"I am your star. I will lead you. When you go to bed, contact me and collect all the accumulated negativity for the day. Put this negativity into your saliva and do not swallow, but spit." "Very well," I said. And the tears flowed down my face. Since then, for over 22 years, I have every night confided my secrets to my star, asked for help in difficult moments of life, and never told anyone about this mysterious communication.

Only when I was 34 did the voice tell me that I could talk about this long association and that I no longer needed to perform the usual ritual. "You have moved to a new level," the Star told me.

It was only later that I learned that this was the constellation of the Pleiades, and the name of my guiding star was Pleione.

In 1992, I was reading a magazine. Because I felt lazy and didn't have much interest, I just skimmed over the lines. I came across Jeane Dixon's prophecy about the coming of the Savior. I am sure that many people certainly heard about this wonderful female prophet, who lived in Washington and associated herself with the powerful elite. She predicted the accession to power of several future Presidents of the United States, the death of John F. Kennedy, the fall of the regime in India, the flight of Americans to the Moon, and many other significant events.

It was only a few lines in a magazine that I read, but what I read sank deep into my consciousness. Suddenly, I could feel an unusual condition A wave of vibration filled my body. Intuitively, I realized that I would find him, the person Dixon spoke of, and that inevitably I would assist in spreading knowledge about which, at that time, I did not have any idea.

I began to wait patiently and to closely monitor information on ordinary people who were born in the Middle East. In the encyclopedia I found countries that were in the Middle East. Many of them. For example: Iran, Israel, Jordan, Kazakhstan, Saudi Arabia and others.

There was no scientist, politician or religious leader who evoked any interest in my heart. I waited patiently, just knowing that I would find this mysterious World Teacher.

Quite unexpectedly for me, my family immigrated to United States in 1998. I remember a mystical moment when, waiting at the U.S. Embassy for my interview, in my head I suddenly heard the voice: "You will live in Boston." But we went to Albany, New York State, where relatives awaited us ... I did not tell anyone about the voice I had heard, but a year after my arrival in the U.S., we moved to Boston and I felt strange support from invisible helpers.

When already living in Boston, in 2004 I stopped by a library and my hand by itself reached for a book entitled A GIFT OF PROPHECY written by Ruth Montgomery. As it happens, the book opened at a page where the vision itself was described in detail.

I would like to state here what exactly that page of the book A GIFT OF PROPHECY revealed to me:

"The vision which Jeane Dixon considers to be the most significant and soul-stirring of her life occurred shortly before sunrise on February 5, 1962. The date itself may have special significance, though Jeane was unaware of that fact at the time. For several months beforehand, astrologers and soothsayers had been predicting an earth-shaking event on that day...some even forecast the end of the world...because of a rare conjunction of the planets. A similar conjunction which occurred nearly two thousand years ago is believed to be by some biblical scholars explaining the "bright star in the East" which dazzled shepherds and guided three Wise Men to a humble manger behind a crowded inn in Bethlehem.

Three nights before Jean's vision she was meditating in her room when she became aware that the light was dimming. Glancing up, she saw the five bulbs in the crystal chandelier go dark, except for a curious round ball which glowed brilliantly in the center of each. Strangely frightened, she ran into her husband's bedroom and told him of the light failure. Since their other house lights were working properly, Mr. Dixon assumed that a fuse for one circuit had blown, but when he went down the hall to investigate, he noticed that Jeane's chandelier was again burning brightly. The next evening during her meditations the phenomenon recurred. This time Jeane remained quietly in her room, staring at the tiny balls of light in the otherwise darkened bulbs. In approximately ten seconds, she says, she heard "a tiny crackling sound." The wires in the clear bulbs then began to glow again, and normal light resumed. When the performance was repeated exactly as before on the third evening, Jeane accepted it as an omen that something important was soon to befall. She did not know when or where. The next morning she overslept, but the sun was not yet up as she walked toward the bay window of her bedroom which faces east.

As she gazed outside she saw, not the bare-limbed trees and city street below, but a bright blue sky above a barren desert. Just above the horizon was the brightest sun that she had ever seen, glowing like a golden ball. Splashing from the orb in every direction were brilliant rays which seemed to be drawing the Earth toward it like a magnet. Stepping out of the brightness of the sun's rays, hand in hand, were a Pharaoh and Queen Nefertiti. Cradled in the Queen's other arm was a baby, his ragged, soled clothing in startling contrast to the gorgeously arrayed royal couple. "The eyes of this child were all-knowing," Jeane said softly. "They were full of wisdom and knowledge."

A little to one side of Queen Nefertiti, Jeane could glimpse a pyramid. While she watched entranced, the couple advanced toward her and thrust forth the baby, as if offering it to the entire world. Within the ball of the sun, Jeane saw Joseph guiding the tableau like a puppeteer pulling strings.

Now rays of light burst forth from the baby, blending with those of the sun and obliterating the Pharaoh from her sight. Off to the left, she observed that Queen Nefertiti was walking away, "thousands of miles into the past." The Queen paused beside a large brown water jug, and as she stooped and cupped her hands to drink she was stabbed in the back by a dagger. Jeane says that she "distinctly heard her death scream as she vanished." Jeane shifted her gaze back to the baby. He had by now grown to manhood, and a small cross which formed above him began to expand until it "dripped over the earth in all directions. Simultaneously, peoples of every race, religion, and color (black, yellow, red, brown and white), each of them kneeling and lifting their arms in worshipful adoration, surrounded him. They were all as one," Unlike previous visions, which had gradually faded away from Jeane, this one moved ever nearer until she seemed to be in the very midst of the action, joining in the adoring worship. "I felt a tiny seed ready to sprout and grow," she says, "But I was only one of millions of similar seeds. I knew within my heart. "Here is the beginning of wisdom" The room was becoming dark again, and though she was still caught up in the spell of the vision, Jeane glanced automatically at her bedside clock. The time was 7:17 a.m.

What does it mean? What is the significance of this strange visitation on a dull February morning in Washington, a third of the way around the world from Egypt/ Jeane feels that she had been shown that answer. A bit haltingly, she explains it this way: "A child, born (will be born?) somewhere in the Middle East shortly after 7 a.m. (EST) on February 5, 1962, will revolutionize the world. Before the close of the century he will bring together all mankind in one all-embracing faith. This will be the foundation of a new Christianity, with every sect and creed united through this man who will walk among the people to spread the wisdom of the Almighty Power.

"This person, though born of humble peasant origin, is a descendant of Queen Nefertiti and her Pharaoh husband; of this I am sure. There was nothing kingly about his coming...no kings or shepherds to do homage to this newborn baby...but he is the answer to the prayers of a troubled world. Mankind will begin to feel the great force of this man in the early 1980's and during the subsequent ten years the world as we know it will be reshaped and revamped into one without wars or suffering. His power will grow greatly until 1999, at which time the people of this earth will probably discover the full meaning of the vision."

Attempting to describe her own sensation, Jeane says: "I felt suspended and enfolded, as if I were surrounded by whipped cream. For the first time I understood the full meaning of the biblical phrase, "My cup runneth over." I loved all mankind. I felt that I would never again need food or sleep, because I had experienced perfect peace."

Jeane died in 1997 without having understood who it was who would save and change this world. While still alive, she repeatedly was mocked by the press precisely because of this prophecy, because she focused on it her entire life. Even Nancy Reagan, close friend and the wife of the former President, did not spare Jeane, and expressed her clear distrust.

Ironic logic prompted the impossibility that someone out there from an Asian area (Chinese or elsewhere?) And he will change the world, but still so young! At that time, the president of Kalmykia Kirsan Ilyumzhinov (born April 5, 1962) is a Kalmyk multi-millionaire businessman and politician, looked very promising, but my heart remained silent with respect to it.

Let me put here a fragment of a curious article, the name is: Out of this world: Russian region leader's alien abduction story shakes officials

The Sydney Morning Gerald, May 6, 2010, you will understand me better. This fact alone shows the unusual character of this gentleman...

"Kirsan Ilyumzhinov says he met creatures in yellow spacesuits. He's a multimillionaire businessman, the leader of the only Buddhist region in Europe, and head of FIDE.

But Kirsan Ilyumzhinov has another claim to fame - he says he was abducted by aliens who landed a spaceship on his balcony in 1997.

Even though 13 years have gone by - including four since The Guardian reported his close encounter of the third kind - he's back in the Earth news big time.

Mr Ilyumzhinov, 48, the head of the south-western Russian region of Kalmykia, appeared on a Russian talk show on April 26, and went over his evening with aliens again.

He said he saw a "semi-transparent half tube" spaceship on his balcony. He then entered it and met "human-like creatures in yellow spacesuits", The Moscow Times reported.

"I am often asked which language I used to talk to them. Perhaps it was on a level of the exchange of the ideas," he told the television program host.

He had told The Guardian the aliens took him to "some kind of star".

"They put a spacesuit on me, told me many things and showed me around. They wanted to demonstrate that UFOs do exist."

What has got his Russian political peers suddenly agitated after all this time is whether he let slip any state secrets and whether there is a proper procedure for dealing with aliens.

Andrei Lebedev, a State Duma deputy, was apparently moved by "holy terror" at Mr Ilyumzhinov's claims, and yesterday wrote to Russian President Dmitry Medvedev asking him to launch an investigation, the Times said.

He was concerned about whether Mr Ilyumzhinov's brush with the spacemen affected his ruling of Kalmykia and whether they might have tried to get him to divulge state secrets to them.

Mr Lebedev also wanted the Russian leader to clarify what guidelines officials were to follow if they were nabbed by aliens.

Glenda Kwek
May 6, 2010»

Years passed, and an abundance of different kinds of psychics, healers, religious leaders - my soul did not assign that special role to anyone. But I lurked and patiently waited for signs of fate, and once, visiting a Russian bookstore, I saw a little book about a mathematics professor, Grigori Grabovoi, and when I read that name, I again had the experience of spontaneous clairvoyance which is not subject to any logical explanation.

"How about that? Here you are and now I've found you," I laughed to myself, completely certain that I was right.

And although I had not read a single work of Grigori Grabovoi at that time, with only the vaguest notions of what it was about, I nevertheless found the opportunity and the courage to officially open a Research Center for the study and spread of the Teachings of Grigori Grabovoi, becoming its president and bookkeeper and secretary all rolled into one. As I understand now one of my reasons why I came to America, is a deciphering of this super important prophecy - and it happened.

I vividly remember a strange moment when I and my family in 1997 were expected at the American Embassy in Moscow calling for an interview, I suddenly heard clearly in my mind the words: "You will live in Boston ..." In my memory there is, as I enveloped the heat and heart beat very fast ... Then it seemed unreal, because we went to New York State, city of Albany, but a year later in 1999, we began to live in New England in Boston. And this point, for me personally, is another striking evidence of nonrandomness happening.

Soon the right people were attracted, and together we already began our study of the Technologies of Consciousness.

Oddly enough, when I reported to Moscow that I had opened the center, I expected that the staff would respond promptly and we would start working in the right direction.

But to my amazement, we were ignored for over a year, as if such Centers in the United States were many.

And when I almost got angry and was tempted to take drastic measures, the document granting us recognition was obtained by allowing those who were engaged in the study to spread the word about the Teachings of Grigori Grabovoi on Eternal and Harmonious Development.

So all these myths about being lured in by a "cult network" seem untenable and unsubstantiated, to say the least, for me and my colleagues.

Soon there occurred another rather unusual event that could be called sensational or miraculous. After finally graduating from nursing school, I had to take the exam in Massachusetts to obtain my hard-earned license. Naturally, I should have put everything else aside to prepare for the exam seriously. But ... in my head there suddenly appeared a bright thought: an order to fly to Moscow urgently. And I felt a strong desire to do it.

Why was I going on this flight? The motivation behind it was weak: just relax, get acquainted with the Moscow group, and if I'm lucky, hear one of the lectures of this teacher Grigori Grabovoi.

I had no idea whether Grigori Grabovoi was in Moscow at this time, and indeed did not possess any more or less intelligible information about the state of affairs.

Easily gathering what I needed in just three days, I saw that the road was opening up before me. No obstacles presented themselves. I was able to buy tickets at a discount. At home, everything was in order. I knew intuitively that the only thing required was not to resist, and to follow the impulse that, more than once, drove me to my destination with no loss of energy.

It was almost nighttime when I arrived at Sheremetyevo Airport and, for personal reasons, I told the taxi driver to take me to any hotel not far from the Alekseevskaya subway station. The taxi driver, somewhat in a hurry and nervous, brought me close to the Exhibition Center subway station, to the hotel Colossus. I was unpleasantly surprised, but it was too late and the taxi driver's behavior had not been what it should have, and so I decided to stay here. The room was nasty, but there was no choice and I went to sleep with great difficulty.

Waking up four hours later than planned, I took a shower and went to look for something more decent and somewhere to have breakfast. My choice fell on the Kosmos Hotel which was located not far away, and I began to climb to the main entrance from the parking lot. The clock showed about twelve o'clock.

I saw a man in a suit who was slowly walking in my direction. There was no one else, either in front of or behind him... Something caused me to watch the approaching man intently. "Looks like Grabovoi," flashed the thought, and I was not mistaken, it was he. We talked quietly for a few minutes, as if the meeting were routine. And we easily resolved the question of a future meeting, because it was necessary to discuss. I had a lot of questions about my activities in the USA. "Sometimes God arranges occasional meetings, and it provides for further development, and this applies to everyone" Grabovoi noted briefly, quoting one of his own lectures.

A great philosopher said :" *Coincidence is God's Secret Language."*

CHAPTER 2

ABOUT GRIGORI GRABOVOI

"Grigori Petrovich Grabovoi was born in November 14, 1963 in BogaRa village, Kirov District, Chimkent Region, Kazakhstan.

He was graduated from the Tashkent State University, faculty of applied mathematics and mechanics, specialty - mechanics, in 1986.

Grigori Grabovoi is a member of the International Academy of Information Sciences, a Corresponding Member of the Russian Academy of Sciences, an advisor to the Russian Federal Aviation Service. He also discovered methods for converting the information contained in any act into a known geometric form. He has identified the principles of remote diagnostics and the regeneration of matter in any time period through the transformation of time into space form. He has been publicly recognized for his unique abilities of clairvoyance, forecasting and treatment. He solves scientific problems using his clairvoyance, and is aware of the result a priori.

He has demonstrated personal abilities of remote control of physical matter from any distance, curing hundreds of diseased persons without being physically present. These facts are certified by traditional medicine and proven by the notarized statements of cured persons.

Grigori Grabovoi has cured multiple persons in the 4th stage of illnesses, and, as certified by the UN, even from 4th-stage AIDS. Using his clairvoyance, he has examined hundreds of aircraft, the "MIR RF" orbital station and the "Atlantis" spacecraft, with his findings absolutely coinciding with what was shown by an actual examination. There are confirming minutes signed by managing and authorized officers of air industry enterprises and the Russian Space Flights Control Center. Under experimental conditions, he performed acts of materialization, de-materialization and teleportation, and these acts were recorded in the minutes. Grigori Grabovoi has regenerated destroyed matter and performs all types of work aimed at the prevention of catastrophes, through creation without destruction. A flow of slanderous misinformation flowed from the pages of the media, from television and the radio onto the heads of unprepared Russians after Grigori Grabovoi announced that he would take upon himself the responsibility for extricating the country from the crisis, and that he intended to be a candidate for President in 2008. It is easy to conjecture that he became a dangerous competitor to other candidates who desire power for their own ambition and so as to be able to retain their wealth, acquired by robbery. Also, as psychologists know, everything new, everything that does not fall within the framework of collective ideas, is always denied at first, and often very aggressively. Time for adjustment is required. This pertains not only to Russia, but the fate of the entire world as well, and it must be clearly understood by all.

Grigori Grabovoi was arrested on April 6, 2006 during a meeting with his followers in the hotel "Cosmos." The charges against him were absurd. Russian courts, under tremendous pressure from the KGB Kremlin Government, pressed groundless and ridiculous criminal charges against Grigori Grabovoi in April of 2006.

I and several people stood with signs near the UN to protect the rights of the great World Teacher Grigori Grabovoi. And then I plucked up courage and protested with placards standing near the White House in Washington. And who knows, maybe it led to a positive result in the further course taken by events. We cannot agree with evil...

Then in 2007 I wrote a letter to Senator Edward M. Kennedy about what was happening. And I got the answer: ...

Dear Mrs. Loginova,

Thank you for your recent correspondence to my office about Mr. Grigori Grabovoi in Russia. I know this matter is concern by you and I sincerely hope I can be of assistance.
I have contacted the Ambassador of Russia in the United States, as well as the State Department , on your behalf. As soon as we receive a response from them, we will be back in touch with you.
Sincerely,

Edward M. Kennedy

The World Teacher has experienced his Calvary too... Great courage is required to spread the Doctrine of Eternal and Harmonious Development. Later I will tell more detail about this terrible and shameful page in history for the Russians. But Mr. Grigori Grabovoi lives in Moscow now and is free. Attorneys and followers have made tremendous efforts to make this happen. Amazing knowledge of the Eternal and Harmonious Development is making its triumphal march around the world. The forces of backwardness and regression were not and are not able to stop this march. ... In this respect, Germany has proved itself as a country open to new knowledge. Today, many lecturers are officially licensed to spread the word of amazing knowledge, holding seminars in the German language. I had the pleasure and honor to hold seminars in Hamburg and Munich in May 2011. I made new friends in Germany who have seen the results and understand the value of the information. I believe that this is a New Science. На сегодняшний момент

The Doctrine of Grigori Grabovoi is spread rapidly around the world. Many licensed teachers in different countries is spread the knowledge of Macro-salvation and humanity's transition to the path of the Eternal and Harmonious Development. This is the United States, France, Australia, Serbia, England, Slovenia, Hungary and other countries. Also a lot of books translated into many languages and change the collective consciousness toward immortality and happiness. Everything happens very quickly on cosmic scale.

Returning to the prediction of Jeane Dixon, she talked about a boy who will change this world for the better, and whose appearance "is an answer to the prayers of a troubled world."

In the book of Elena Muhovikova, physician from Kazakhstan, she describes her meeting with Grigori Grabovoi's mother, who provided interesting information about her unusual son:

«Grigori knew from early childhood what the goal of his appearance on the planet was. As a three-year-old child, Grigori saw the threat of destruction that hung over the Earth. He clearly saw the sufferings of people, wars, epidemics, ruin. But how he could help at this age? Being hidden in a secluded place where nobody could disturb him, the little boy, by an effort of his will, mentally placed the globe in his heart, and saw an infinite stream of love relieving the strain of the planet, preventing it from breaking up and bringing people calm. Already at the age of three, Grigori repeated to adults that it was necessary to rescue the planet. He astounded relatives with his strange statements and out-of-the-ordinary abilities. His mother Ludmila Ilinichna tried to hide her son's ability from others to keep them from being shocked.

Grandmother Claudia Ivanovna, of noble heritage, was born into an aristocratic family and she took Grigori under her care.

Grigori Grabovoi's mother reported to Elena Muhovikova an interesting vignette from the life of her extraordinary son.

Grigori grew up to be a quiet boy; he never raised his voice at anyone, no shouting, no fighting and was perfectly healthy. He had no medical records because he was never ill. Grigori had no vaccinations, and never saw a doctor.

When the boy was five years old, his parents decided to show him to a clairvoyant old man, a Muslim, who lived in another village 20 km away. Ludmila Ilinichna tells: "When we entered his yard, the clairvoyant's son started to say that his father was 80 years old and did not receive any visitors because he was old and weak. We had already turned around and were about to leave, but we were stopped by the shout of this clairvoyant, who demanded that the Russian boy be brought to him. "We parents were asked to stay in the yard. A long agonizing hour of waiting passed before Grigori re-appeared. "What was he doing with you for so long?" asked Lyudmila Ilinichna. "Nothing - Grigori answered. "He fell to his knees in front of me, kissed my hand, my forehead, and then prayed for an hour. After that, Grandfather got up and again kissed my hands, forehead and told me to now invite you in to see him. "

When the parents saw the old man again, he solemnly asked them if they know that their son has been born of God? Ludmila Ilinichna confirmed this with a nod. The Muslim seer continued: "Your son is a child conceived by God, and not a single hair on his head should be harmed. Keep him as the apple of your eye, and do not show him to anyone. The boy has excellent health. If someone dares to offend him, then a curse will fall on seven tribes." Remembering the guidance of the clairvoyant, Grigori's grandmother became his main guardian. She accompanied him everywhere."

My profession in Russia was as an engineer of explosive materials, a mechanical engineer in chemical production. Ironically, fate has made me an American nurse, and I have the possibility of observing literal horrors, where the person is transformed by illnesses and old age. I have no doubt that aging is an unnatural state for people. Old age is a humiliating, sad and ugly disease.

A few times, as people lay dying, I saw the moment when they left. I looked with interest, as a researcher seeking to understand something. And I once realized why this was shown to me! We need to understand a very important thing: Mankind has lost its way.... What is happening is not right and we urgently need to change the situation. Man has the ability to set his/her own laws in nature and physics. I know it sounds strange, but it is nonetheless reality. A good illustration of this is the ability to levitate or teleport. The New Science, once it becomes the norm, will become part of man's collective consciousness. The New Science is essentially a new direction of knowledge, confirming a way of development only in the direction of the world's creative, positive development.

For the first time it has been mathematically proven that, if you change your perceptions, it is possible to transform the information in all systems of a reality.

Grabovoi is one of the few scientists who can think globally. His name is included in the list of names that make up the intellectual elite of Russia. The Goal of the Teaching is Harmonious Salvation of all and every person, the maintenance of Eternal Creative Harmonious Development.
Using the Technology of Consciousness in the manner of the Creator, Grigori Grabovoi has proved that even such diseases as cancer and AIDS in the last stage can be cured. He teaches all people of the world the use of the Technologies of Salvation, and our goal is to teach them to save ourselves and others.
Grigori Grabovoi never prepares a lecture in advance. The theme and the information appear at the moment when he begins to speak before an audience. I attended one of Grabovoi's lectures, and had the impression that he spoke not like a man of today, but a Man of the Future.

He regularly repeats his credo: "Any event can be changed. My forecasts are not fated. I am always looking for a constructive method of forestalling. I do not change the object; I am changing the situation around it."

The lectures of Grigori Grabovoi are not simple to grasp, , even for a well-prepared person. But the followers are continuing with the work, and all goes well. All teaching is permeated by a quite positive energy, without coyness or manipulation. WHEN you become aware of even a part of the information from the lectures, then you begin to feel that human beings are Godlike; you begin to feel joy and hope. But also responsibility. Any person has free will. NOBODY HAS THE RIGHT TO DICTATE to another. You can only transfer knowledge. It is necessary to form a new collective consciousness so that we can cure all: you can cure cancer, AIDS, cirrhosis of the liver, grow back teeth that have been pulled. A person does not have the disease in his canonical form. A disease is external information. Somewhere, inside the object, you are missing information that corresponds to a healthy you.

Grigori Grabovoi has created the Technology to prevent man-made disasters, as well as the Technology for radical life extension. He has been awarded the highest state award of Bulgaria - the Order of Stara Planina, 1st class, "because an accident at the Kozloduy nuclear power plant in Bulgaria was prevented in 1999.

The main goal of human life is to raise the level of his consciousness.

The personal consciousness of each person is a component of the collective consciousness of all humans which is very powerful as it operates across all humanity. We must change Collective Consciousness to direction Eternal Harmonious Development.

I am sure that the appearance on Earth of Grigori Grabovoi can help humanity avoid a third, nuclear world war. The future always has multiple outcomes. Let's choose a bright future, an eternal and harmonious development!

CHAPTER 3

THE GRAND LAMA DJWHAL KHUL ABOUT THE IMMINENT SECOND COMING OF THE SAVIOR IN VISIBLE FORM

I want to extend in more detail on the personality Djwhal Khul, the lama of all lamas, not a mythical person, but a particular Teacher who was a master in telepathic abilities, allowing him to dictate Alice Bailey's book in 1947, a document entitled " The Reappearance of the Christ".

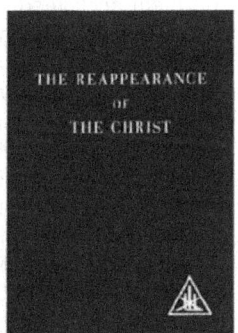

The Tibetan

EXTRACT FROM A STATEMENT BY THE TIBETAN
Djwhal Khul, through Alice A. Bailey (1934)

"Suffice it to say, that I am a Tibetan disciple of a certain degree, and this tells you but little, for all are disciples, from the humblest aspirant up to, and beyond, the Christ Himself. I live in a physical body like other men, on the borders of Tibet, and at times (from the exoteric standpoint) preside over a large group of Tibetan lamas, when my other duties permit. It is this fact that has caused it to be reported that I am an abbot of this particular lamasery. Those associated with me in the work of the Hierarchy (and all true disciples are associated in this work) know me by still another name and office. Alice A. Bailey knows who I am and recognises me by two of my names. I am a brother of yours, who has travelled a little longer upon the Path than has the average student, and has therefore incurred greater responsibilities. I am one who has wrestled and fought his way into a greater measure of light than the aspirant who will read this article, and I must therefore act as a transmitter of the light, no matter what the cost. I am not an old man, as age counts among the teachers, yet I am not young or inexperienced. My work is to teach and spread the knowledge of the Ageless Wisdom wherever I can find a response, and I have been doing this for many years. I seek also to help the Master M. and the Master K.H. whenever opportunity offers, for I have been long connected with Them and with Their work. In all of the above, I have told you much; yet at the same time I have told you nothing which would lead you to offer me that blind obedience and the foolish devotion which the emotional aspirant offers to the Guru and Master Whom he is yet unable to contact. Nor will he make that desired contact until he has transmuted emotional devotion into unselfish service to humanity--not to the Master.

The books I have written are sent out with no claim for their acceptance. They may, or may not, be correct, true and useful. It is for you to ascertain their truth by right practice and by the exercise of the intuition. Neither I nor A.A.B. is the least interested in having them acclaimed as inspired writings, or in having anyone speak of them (with bated breath) as being the work of one of the Masters. If they present truth in such a way that it follows sequentially upon that already offered in the world teachings, if the information given raises the aspiration and the will-to-serve from the plane of the emotions to that of the mind (the plane whereon the Masters can be found), then they will have served their purpose. If the teaching conveyed calls forth a response from the illumined mind of the worker in the world, and brings a flashing forth of his intuition, then let that teaching be accepted. But not otherwise. If the statements meet with eventual corroboration, or are deemed true under the test of the Law of Correspondences, then that is well and good. But should this not be so, let not the student accept what is said. (August 1934) "

"Right down the ages, in many world cycles and in many countries (and today in all) great points of tension have occurred which have been characterized by a hopeful sense of expectancy. Some one is expected and His coming is anticipated. Always in the past, it has been the religious teachers of the period who have fostered and proclaimed this expectancy and the time has always been one of chaos and difficulty, of a climaxing point at the close of a civilization or culture and when the resources of the old religions have seemed inadequate to meet men's difficulties or to solve their problems. The coming of the Avatar, the advent of a Coming One and, in terms of today, the reappearance of the Christ is the keynotes of the prevalent expectancy. When the times are ripe, the invocation of the masses is strident enough and the faith of those who know is keen enough, then always He has come and today will be no exception to this ancient rule or to this universal law. For decades, the reappearance of the Christ, the Avatar, has been anticipated by the faithful in both hemispheres - not only by the Christian faithful, but by those who look for Maitreya and for the Boddhisattva as well as those who expect the Imam Mahdi."

"In any acceptance of the teaching that Christ will come, one of the difficulties today is the feeling that the teaching has been given for many centuries and nothing has ever happened. That is a statement of fact, and here lies a great deal of our trouble. The expectancy of His coming is nothing new; in it lies nothing unique or different; those who still hold to the idea are regarded tolerantly, or with amusement or pity, as the case may be."

"He will come to a world which is essentially one world. His reappearance and His consequent work cannot be confined to one small locality or domain unheard of by the great majority, as was the case when He was here before. The radio, the press and the dissemination of news will make His coming different to that of any previous Messenger; the swift modes of transportation will make Him available to countless millions, and by boat, rail and plane they can reach Him: through television, His face can be made familiar to all, and verily "every eye shall see Him." Even if there is no general recognition of His spiritual status and His message, there must necessarily be a universal interest, for today even the many false Christs and Messengers are finding this universal curiosity and cannot be hidden. This creates a unique condition in which to work, and one which no salvaging, energizing Son of God has ever before had to face."

..."The sensitivity of the people of the world to what is new or needed is also uniquely different; man has progressed far in his reaction to both good and evil and possesses a far more sensitive response apparatus than did humanity in those earlier times. If there was a quick response to the Messenger when He came before, it will be more general and quicker now, both in rejection and in acceptance. Men are more enquiring, better educated, more intuitive and more expectant of the unusual and the unique than at any other time in history. Their intellectual perception is keener, their sense of values more acute, their ability to discriminate and choose is fast developing, and they penetrate more quickly into significances. These facts will condition the reappearance of the Christ and tend to a more rapid spreading of the news of His coming and the contents of His message."

..."Today, when He comes, He will find a world uniquely free from the grip and hold of ecclesiasticism; when He came before, Palestine was held in the vicious grasp of the Jewish religious leaders, and the Pharisees and the Sadducees were to the people of that land what the potentates of the church are to the people in the world today. But - there has been a useful and wholesome swing away from Churchianity and from orthodox religion during the past century, and this will present a unique opportunity for the restoration of true religion and the presentation of a simple return to the ways of spiritual living. The priests, the Levites, the Pharisees and the Sadducees were not the ones who recognized Him when He came before. They feared Him. And it is highly improbable that the reactionary churchmen will be the ones to recognize Him today. He may reappear in a totally unexpected guise; who is to say whether He will come as a politician, an economist, a leader of the people (arising from the midst of them), a scientist or an artist?"

"It is a fallacy to believe, as some do, that the main trend of Christ's work will be through the medium of the churches or the world religions. He necessarily will work through them when conditions permit and there is a living nucleus of true spirituality within them, or when their invocative appeal is potent enough to reach Him. He will use all possible channels whereby the consciousness of man may be enlarged and right orientation be brought about. It is, however, truer to say that it is as World Teacher that He will consistently work, and that the churches are but one of the teaching avenues He will employ. All that enlightens the minds of men, all propaganda that tends to bring about right human relations, all modes of acquiring real knowledge, all methods of transmuting knowledge into wisdom and understanding, all that expands the consciousness of humanity and of all subhuman states of awareness and sensitivity, all that dispels glamour and illusion and that disrupts crystallization and disturbs static conditions will come under the realistic activities of the Hierarchy which He supervises. He will be limited by the quality and the caliber of the invocative appeal of humanity and that, in its turn, is conditioned by the attained point in evolution."

"Humanity in all lands today awaits the Coming One - no matter by what name they may call Him. The Christ is sensed as on His way. The second coming is imminent and, from the lips of disciples, mystics, aspirants, spiritually-minded people and enlightened men and women, the cry goes up, "Let light and love and power and death fulfill the purpose of the Coming One." These words are a demand, a consecration, a sacrifice, a statement of belief and a challenge to the Avatar, the Christ, Who waits in His high place until the demand is adequate and the cry clear enough to warrant His appearance."

CHAPTER 4

THE MICHEL NOSTRADAMUS ABOUT THE COMING OF THE MESSIAH

Michel Nostradamus (1503-1566) was the greatest prophet in the last millennium. He is the best known and most accurate mystic and seer of all times. There are those who say that he predicted Napoleon and even the attack on the World Trade Center. Read the prophecies and judge for yourself. We learn that Michel Nostradamus was a healer, an apothecary and a physician who lost his family to plague and became a dabbler in dark arts. He combined elements of Judaeo-Christian sources with astrology, the occult and study of the ancients to produce works that became best-sellers. In his "histories of the future" he made predictions about events as far ahead as the year 3797. His immense popularity in his day makes Nostradamus perhaps the world's first author to make a fortune writing science fiction.
However, Michel Nostradamus is best known as author of the "Centuries" ("Century"), published first in 1555, and since reprinted many times.
In this prophetic book of rhymed quatrains (quatrains) encoded the coming events in France, in Europe, in Russia and in the world.
Since my study concerns Grigori Grabovoi, a Russian citizen, it is very interesting to follow what thought the great clairvoyant about this long-suffering country. Despite the fact that Nostradamus frankly did not like all of Russia for the acts of Russians in different centuries, he still envied those who would live in the Russian land after 500 years after his death. Why? It becomes clear after reading the prophecies. But we will look carefully at the information that points to the coming of the Messiah; the man who will change the world today.

Long awaited he will never return
In Europe, he will appear in Asia:
One of the leagued issued from the great Hermes,
And he will grow over all the Kings of the East.
  (Centurie 10 Q 75)

The law of the Sun and of Venus in strife,
Appropriating the spirit of prophecy:
Neither the one nor the other will be understood,
The law of the great Messiah will hold through the Sun.
  (Centurie 5 Q 53)

The sacred pomp will come to lower its wings,
Through the coming of the Great Legislator:
He will raise the humble. He will vex the rebels,
His like will not appear on this Earth.
  (Centurie 5 Q 79)

The Moon in the full of night over the high mountain,
The new sage with a lone brain has seen it:
By his disciples invited to be immortal,
Eyes to the south.
Hands in bosoms, bodies in the fire.
  (Centurie 4 Q 31)

The body without soul
No longer to be sacrificed:
Day of birth put for birthday:
The divine spirit will make the soul happy,
Seeing the World in its Eternity.
  (Centurie 2Q 13)

Temples consecrated in the original Roman manner,
They will reject the excess foundations,
Taking their first and humane laws,
Chasing, though not entirely, the cult of saints.
  (Centurie 2 Q 8)

The Prince rare in pity and mercy
Will come to change through death great knowledge:
Through great tranquility the realm attended to,
When the great one
Soon will be fleeced.
  (Centurie 7 Q 17)

Born in the shadow and during a dark day,

He will be sovereign in realm and goodness:
He will cause his blood to rise again in the ancient urn,
Renewing the age of gold
For that of brass.
(Centurie 5 Q 41)

Where did Michel Nostradamus draw information from? He claimed that he received the knowledge of future events from the Holy Spirit. Even Michel Nostradamus claimed that the future is multiple and the free will of man is able to change any of the events.He said: "I have also in mind that the future is definitely not the final, and whatever all over the reigns and governs all the power of the Almighty God ... Some things will only get inspired by God and divine inspiration."

In one of his books the famous scientist, cosmist Vadim Chernobrov is as follows:

"If the future is determined, what's the point report that still needs to happen and this can not be changed? Who said that the future is fixed and predictably? ... Nostradamus did not say, just an incredible accuracy of the prophecy has led many people to make premature conclusions. However, the essence of prophecy comes down to what we can not only change our future, but we should do it, unless, of course, we want to live in a normal world, not to drown in the third world flood of human blood."

I propose to consider carefully the fragment of the famous open Letter to King Henry II of France by Nostradamus:

"Then the great Empire of the Antichrist will begin where once was Attila's empire and the new Xerxes will descend with great and countless numbers, so that the coming of the Holy Ghost, proceeding from the 48th degree, will make a transmigration, chasing out the abomination of the Christian Church, and whose reign will be for a time and to the end of time. This will be preceded by a solar eclipse more dark and gloomy than any since the creation of the world, except that after the death and passion of Jesus Christ. And it will be in the month of October than the great translation will be made and it will be such that one will think the gravity of the earth has lost its natural movement and that it is to be plunged into the abyss of perpetual darkness. In the spring there will be omens, and thereafter extreme changes, reversals of realms and mighty earthquakes. These will be accompanied by the procreation of the new Babylon, miserable daughter enlarged by the abomination of the first holocaust. It will last for only seventy-three years and seven months."

Next comes the arrival of the World Teacher: "Then there will issue from the stock which had remained barren for so long, proceeding from the 50th degree, one who will renew the whole Christian Church. Great pease will be established, with union and concord between some of the children of opposite ideas, who have been seperated by diverse realms. And such will be the peace that the instigator and promoter of military factions, born of the diversity of religions, will remain chained to the deepest pit. And the

kingdom of the Furious One, who counterfeits the sage, will be united. "
Many researchers have tried to unravel who was this man, but I think my epiphany is the right thing! And I will prove it easily: almost directly in the center of Kazakhstan passes 50 latitude. In this Asian country is the intersection of 50 latitude and 50 longitude. Kazakhstan is the country in which Grigori Grabovoi was born. Do you know many personalities of such magnitude born in Kazakhstan?

Two well-known Russian researchers Dmitry and Nadezda Zima, found the codes to decipher the quatrains and I believe them. After reviewing many others, and not only by Russian researchers, where, in my opinion, is *"pulling events in the ears"*, these two have come really close ... Dmitry and Nadezda found the code 11.11 and 36, 72. They calculated the two dates, taking the quatrain:

The year 1999, seventh month,
From the sky will come a great King of Terror:
To bring back to life the great King of the Angolmoise,
Before and after Mars to reign by good fortune.
(Centurie X Q 72)

Nostradamus often used duration in two ways: placing the code in the opposite direction from the reference point. The Prophet simply has placed from 1999 year the period of 36 years: the period "before and after Mars' means the period from 1963 to 2035 (Note - the number of quatrain 72). Dmitriy and Nadezda Zima claim that 2035 is the year of transition to a new state of humanity (this is the same in Kabbalah and astrology). But they shyly apologize for the date in 1963! They said, sorry, we do not know where it came from and what it means, but the correctness of the calculations, these researchers are absolutely sure!

I know the answer: 1963 is the year of birth of Grigori Grabovoi, who brought radically new and powerful Technologies of Rescue. Incidentally, in 1999 is the year when Grigori Grabovoi save the world from global catastrophe, to prevent a nuclear explosion at the Kozloduy plant in Bulgaria. Many of the great seers point to this year, as a possible global catastrophe (Edgar Cayce, Jeane Dixon, Nostradamus, aliens, different religions and many others).

This quatrain refers to the "King of intimidation ..." Not only I, but other independent researchers have drawn attention to the fact that it was in 1999 that came to power Vladimir Putin. Indeed, Putin was appointed Prime Minister, August 9, 1999, was elected President of Russia in March 2000. March 2008 (the Constitution) was the last month of his presidency. The coincidence is even more accurate, given that Nostradamus everywhere indicates the date on the Julian calendar in effect in France in the XVI century. Dates on this calendar are different from the modern Gregorian ten days, so Vladimir Putin in the coordinate system of Nostradamus becomes Prime Minister exactly after seven months of 1999, as indicated in the quatrain 10.72. I will not pursue the matter, think for yourself.

CHAPTER 5

INTERESTING THINGS SAID BY WELL-KNOWN RUSSIAN CLAIRVOYANT, YURI KRETOV

In Russia, I highlighted a few clairvoyant. I found an interesting one, Mr. Yuri Kretov, who is director of the theater in Dillon St. Petersburg. Extraordinary personality: independent, unusual perceptions of reality and, at least until 2005, was honest in his statements...

I do not know him personally, but I know a serious man who met him and had him interviewed. I do not like some things that this clairvoyant says. Too much attention is given to such things as death, but I would like to hear more about life without death...

Yuri Kretov foretold the death of President Boris Yeltsin to the day; he was invited to certain services in the U.S. providing all conditions for a dignified life. But Yuri Kretov prefers the independence of any formal structures. Here is a fragment from a conversation with him published in the newspaper "NEW PETERBURG", № 33 (744), 08/18/2005 was:

" You have repeatedly been offered the best deals. Why do you refuse them?

-In 1991 I was visited by representatives from Philadelphia, from the military hospital, and within a month they urged me to go with them. Question even agreed with the American Embassy. However, I chose to stay here, in Russia, with my theater. At the same time came messengers from Raisa Gorbachev. During the week, urged me to move to Moscow. In the first case I was scared that I would be restricted to travel abroad from the United States, the second - was afraid to approach close to power, because power pulls a huge plume of bindings, obligations, and promises. I prefer to be free.

- Do you still consult the powers that be? Many of them are at risk and fearful for their health and their lives. Are you sure that would help them, for example, to be warn about the danger?

- It's real. But as I said: be careful. "

Who will stop "doomsday"?

Interview with Yuri Cretov, clairvoyant, healer, Theater Director "Diklon" living in St. Petersburg, Russia.

   - Last time a lot of noise around the name of Grigori Grabovoi. What is really going on and why these attacks from the press?
   - I would recommend to be careful with Grabovoi. Before the "sling mud at him," remember that he once was called a dirty crook of Jesus Christ. Once removed Grigori Rasputin, who predicted many things that later turned out to be true. Before the "blather" and "caw", it is necessary to understand the situation and who is who. From my point of view, Grabovoi is the very serious figure. A more serious person in the world today I do not see.
   - Capable of Grigori Grabovoi affect some events?
   - Capable. He does not require any evidence. His function he performs brilliantly. We should be grateful at least for what will happen in 2012. As a result of displacement of the magnetic poles of the globe, there will be very unpleasant things. But Grabovoi will save the situation. I suggest you look at these pictures, which I tried to depict what is happening on our planet in 2012.

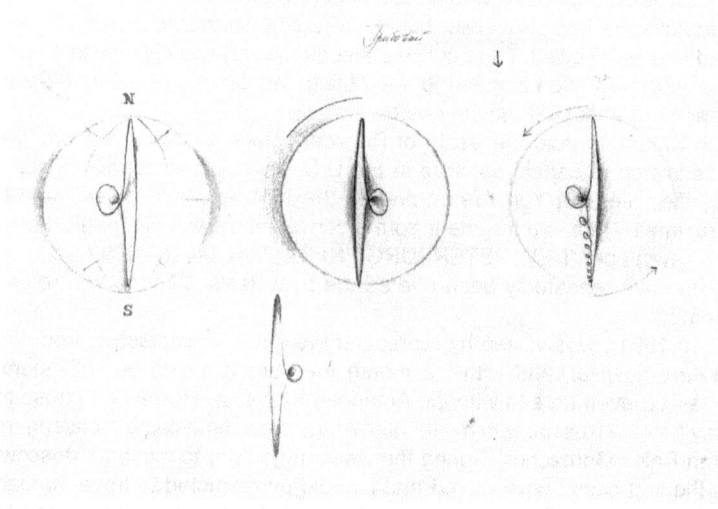

What should happen to be and will not happen - it's all Grabovoi.
   - Do you think that if the world did not die and not go crazy, that's all - Grabovoi?
   - Yes it is. If Vanga was alive now and we would refer to her with the question, who is Grabovoi, she would have said: "There will come a cutter

and it will solve the problem." Perhaps someday we will have a monument with the inscription: "From the grateful inhabitants of the Earth to Grigori Petrovich Grabovoi."

- Well, let's say it is. Then how do you explain all negative, all this hype around the name of Grabovoi? Are you aware of upcoming events that people at the top do not know?

They know. It is highly significant that recently came to me one of the authorities, and I gave evidence of what will happen to the planet. Ironically, this date is already known to our authorities. Most likely, the noise in the media is greatly associated with political overtones. Organizers of a smear campaign against Grabovoi know perfectly well why they do it. To cut the branch on which they sit, I would not recommend them."

And here a fragment of a conversation of Yuri Kretov with another journalist confirming previous:

"Kretov: Twice I saw the planet. When I saw Grabovoi, I saw the planet. And when I asked what would happen in December 2012. Then I saw the planet. Two times. Only twice. December 23, and saw with Grabovoi. And so on I can say is do not bring a claim to this man because he is a very important tool for something. And do not go "poke your nose." No need to lash out...

CHAPTER 6

GRIGORI RASPUTIN - THE FORERUNNER OF THE ARRIVAL OF THE SAVIOR?

"At the time of the sunset you will see miracles and suffering. But you also see the kingdom of shadows in the likeness of men. Keep your eyes on the East because there will come new prophets. They will prepare a way for the Lord, who is also in the glare coming from the East."

"Grigori Rasputin".

Someone great said: "Coincidences are God's language." Based on the fact that the Russian language has multidimensional and demiurgic meaning, I propose to consider carefully the meaning inherent in the name of the Russian seer and prophet.

The name of the seer - GRIGORI. Subconsciously, a philistine does not bother to excessive perturbation of the brain and soul, connects the name with the name of Grigori Grabovoi with Grigori Rasputin. And here, I think, gets the bull's-eye!

Grigori Rasputin, in my opinion, is the forerunner of the Messiah, as was the case with John the Baptist two millennia ago. There is a tragic analogy of these two historical figures: violent death at the hands of those in power and abuse is already a dead body. Was there more sacred and meaningful prophet in Russia than Grigori Rasputin? I doubt it.

The secret police had fabricated almost a copy of the great visionary, and used it to create a negative image to manipulate and achieve their dirty goals. For example, Grigori Rasputin was against war with Germany and spoke about it to Tsar Nicholas the Second, but some forces that are interested precisely in the conduct of hostilities, have developed a detailed plan to discredit and destroy Rasputin. Him true saint, slandered and killed However, it should be noted, the effect of such gentlemen as noble Usupov, was also predicted very accurately by visionary without options: almost instantaneous disappearance of the nobility as a class, a terrible civil war and the flood of human blood in Russia for a long, long time ... Here it is the role of the individual in history!

If you're curious, I recommend the memoirs of Rasputin's daughter, Matrona, who died in 1977 while living in the United States.

So, returning to the interpretation of the name of Grigori Rasputin we have the following: Grigori Ra-s-putin, a certain person who carries in his last name the symbolism of God of Sun RA, will be manifested in the world, with Putin's rule. ("S" means in Russian like "with") Messiah GRIGORI (bring the light of knowledge, this knowledge as the light will illuminate the path of humanity RA) RA s (with) Putin.By the way, I carried out a thorough investigation of the life of King Herod and Mr. Vladimir Putin. The parallels are just impressive! In general, the God of Sun RA will live at the same time with Putin. We are always given the signs; you just have to learn to read properly ... This helps spiritual growth, inner freedom and intuition.

I will not repeat as much genius and progressive people have passed through the prison. Gray and black individuals can not tolerate light, illuminating their greyness and blackness. But before you change something, we must see the problem and change quickly to merge with the Light! "I come as the Light (Lightning, in another translation, the Light of Knowledge of God.) and everyone will see me." - Jesus said.

I want to give some of the prophecies of St. Grigori Rasputin, the Siberian, which are speaking for themselves.

"When the times come close to the abyss, the love of a man turn into a dry plant. In the wilderness of those days will grow only two plants - the plant of profit and the plant of selfishness. But the flowers of these plants can be mistaken for the flowers of love. All of humanity will be absorbed by the indifference. Few people and few things will remain, but what will remain will be required to undergo a new purification before entering into a new earthly paradise. "

Even back in 1913, Grigori Rasputin predicted the start date of World War II, the blockade of Leningrad and the victory of Russia. One day Rasputin, angry at a German asylum, said: "I know that surrounds St. Petersburg, hunger will starve. Lord, how many people will die! And some bread to not see the palm. But you can not see St. Petersburg! Die of hunger, and not let the enemy. And it is from my death - the 25th year."

Blockade of Leningrad began in 1941. Rasputin is known to have been killed December 17, 1916. In 1913, Rasputin predicted the landing of Americans on the moon: "Americans walk on the moon will leave your shameless flag and fly away. They are in boxes, and boast that they jump on us. But you do not worry, be the first to Jura. And not on the Moon but in heaven. "

(Yura is the first astronaut Yuri Gagarin. Author's Note)

The most well known prophecy of Rasputin that he made shortly before his death, "Letter to Nicholas II":

"If the Russian peasants will kill me, then you, Russian Tsar, do not fear anyone. Stay on the throne, and reign. If I will be killed nobles and gentry, then the following happens: the brothers turn against brother, and they will kill each other for 25 years. If your relatives commit murder, none of your family, that is, children and relatives do not live longer than two years. They were soon killed. "

The strength of Rasputin, his gift of the seer was evident to his contemporaries, even the standard of morality John of Kronstadt called Rasputin "Wanderer, having the gift of prayer."

Felix Yusupov, a relative of the king and assassin of Rasputin said, "I can assure you that people like Rasputin, with the magnetic force are once every few centuries."

"No one can replace Rasputin, so we must eliminate Rasputin and this will have good consequences for the revolution."

All predictions later came true. And God forbid fulfilled another prophecy of Grigori Rasputin, which was made in October 1916, shortly before his death. "the elder". "Grigori has asked me to remember for a lifetime what he says: " Remember. Was Russia - will be a red pit. There was a red pit - will swamp the wicked, which have dug a red pit. It was a swamp with the wicked, but there will be a dry field, but will no longer be Russia - there will be no pit. I asked why it said: "To know that I will not see."

Transcribe too easy, but hard on my soul.

However, the prophet is still very optimistic on the ending of the battle.

"Skip spark that will bring a New Word and a New Law. And the New Law will teach people a new life. Because in the new house will not be able to enter the old habits. And when the sun set, it appears that the New Law is the ancient law, and man was created under the Law."

CHAPTER 7

Vanga said to Grigori Grabovoi:
"You are God! You will save the world!"

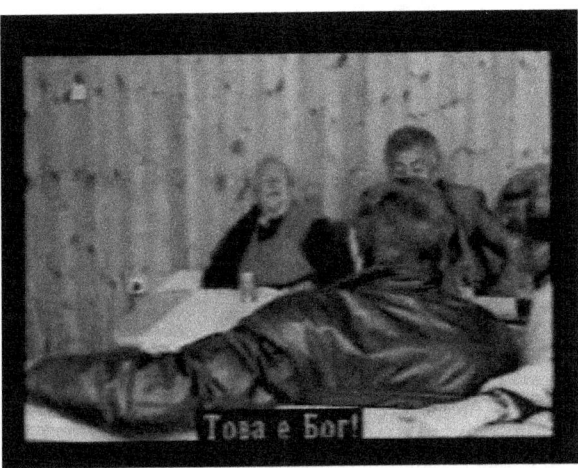

Among world famous psychics is well known Bulgarian seer Vanga and her prophecies which have come true by a large percentage. And indeed her work with information to certain people inspires confidence.

The Russian media are not lazy and did a great job of distorting the words of Vanga, which she said, when she had a meeting with Grigori Grabovoi in 1995. I will not dwell on it, but I want to draw your attention to several times repeated the phrase, addressed to Grigori Grabovoi, whose the meaning of which was that Herod on Earth right now and is very close to him. "Fear of Herod the king!" - Literally screaming clairvoyant. She also noted that for 20 years (we are talking about 1995) Grigori Grabovoi perform all tasks undertaken. In the video posted titles, which are written in Bulgarian, and the meeting itself filmed by an independent Bulgarian TV. We read the following words: "You are the one whose name is God!"

Genkova Valentine, director of the film, says that in her film about Vanga were changed (tampered with) comments. Vanga spoke with Grigori Grabovoi about 50 minutes. They talked about saving the world.

Here are a few of the prophecies Vanga made before meeting with Grigori Grabovoi.

"Humanity is on the path to insanity. And this thirst for power and the violence. But how is it - yesterday's criminals have people run? Deception, perversion, infidelity, ... The fact that people cling to evil, as opposed to what is good - all of them back, it hurts to come back. "

"Unbelieving man hard to help - remember this!"

"More and more often you'll meet people who have eyes but do not see, ears, but do not hear. Brother against brother goes; the mother will abandon their children. Everyone will find a way to escape alone. Some of them get rich, but people will become poor, more and worse. Many diseases appear, people will start dying off like flies ..."

"The day will come when a lie will disappear from the face of the earth. There will be no violence and theft. All wars will stop; the survivors will know the price of life and will defend it. "

In May 1979, Vanga predicted that "The world will survive many disasters and powerful shocks. Consciousness of people will change drastically. There will be a difficult time. People are divided on the basis of faith. But at last return to the planet's oldest and wisest Teaching."

"People ask me: - Vanga said, -" when the time is? "Not soon! Even Syria has not fallen." (R. Stoyanova, "Vanga: confession of blind clairvoyant").

CHAPTER 8

Nol van Valer about the Second Coming of Jesus Christ

It was the first time I got into a small, but very unusual town called Mt. Shasta in October 2010. The town is located a few miles from the beautiful and mysterious Mount Shasta. At the will of fate the second time I arrived there in early December 2011. The purpose was to hold a seminar in English.

At this time tourists are almost not coming, because if the snow goes, and sometimes it drops so much that the house is submerged, it gets extremely difficult and even dangerous. So I was not even really sure that someone would come. But me and this option is arranged, as the call and gravity were stronger than all rational arguments.

And I was rewarded for the risk. There were a few people, but they were behind great spiritual achievements and attracted them was the desire to learn new things and then share with others.... We became friends and did not disappoint each other.

What kind of opening I want to tell? The fact is that even the very esoteric Mt. Shasta residents developed or have not heard anything, or very superficially know about a woman named Nola Van Valer.

The fate of Nola and her husband are very unusual and I want to briefly write how it all began. She wrote two small books that are somewhat a rarity now.

It was, as far as I could discern, in early 1930.

Nola and her husband Jerry lived at the time in the city of San Jose.

One day Jerry came back from one of the cities on the West Coast, where he underwent a medical examination for heart disease, which, as the doctors said, was for him not curable, was serious and the doctors said that does not help. Standing on the platform of a railway station in Salt Lake City, he met a priest of the Orthodox Greek in a black cassock and a high black hat. On his breast hung a thick chain with a huge cross.

This strange priest for those places with a long beard, approached Jerry and told him that there where he was going to make a connection, big snow fell and the train stood for a long time that he had better go to another train in Mount Shasta, and then Jerry is late home quite a bit. . It was amazing because no one knew exactly where he went. Once he still changed his ticket and went to his compartment, next to his amazement, the priest was sitting there, on the contrary.

They talked and told the priest that they will pass through Northern California by Mount Shasta, which Jerry had never heard before, and that the inhabitants of a small town sometimes see a strange, mysterious glow. Then the conductor confirmed that once the train stopped to see how the light and suddenly the driver saw on tracks a huge stone boulder. If not stopped, the catastrophe would be inevitable.

The priest again very surprised Jerry saying that he knew of his serious and incurable disease and it can be cured with the help of his older brother. He said that if Jerry will make a stop in Mt.Shasta, it will soon be a real help. Jerry hesitated, and when the train arrived at the station, he just decided to go for a minute, leaving his hat and coat in the compartment. Near the station, he saw there was a huge and very beautiful limousine with a chauffeur, which had never seen before and thought that only very rich people can afford such a machine.

The priest suddenly invited to sit in a limousine and chauffeur dropped the phrase: "Sit down, I'm waiting for you." They went pretty far down the bumpy road, and when passed through a certain station, then Jerry asked to stop to go to the toilet. When he came back, the limousine had disappeared with the priest and his driver. But there was a white horse-drawn carriage with in what is unusual, an ancient style, and there was a man of the eastern type (Chinese, Tibetan?) Who asked him to sit down and explained that they would have to go for some time. Jerry had neither coat nor hat and mentally thought, not whether he go crazy! But he did not feel the cold!

They came closer to the night when the sky was starred in a very beautiful form of Tibetan house.

In this unusual, eastern house was burning a fireplace. Soon, a man brought a hot meal, which was a vegetable soup. Very tasty and hearty, that suddenly filled the pilgrim life-giving energy and power. The man who brought the food was presented, as Long Mol. Strange, but Jerry felt that he knew him.... He was told to relax, rest, and then surely meet his elder brother of the priest. After a rest, Maul Long said that we should take some distance on foot and then the guest mentally again was horrified that the men would freeze in their shoes and no one ever would find his body until the snow melts.

But he didn't feel cold for no apparent reason!

Then describes the strange scene as Jerry fell asleep and then woke up when the pier Long told him that it was time to meet his elder brother. They went on foot for approximately half a mile into the woods and the way the moonlight. All around were beautiful pine trees. Suddenly, next to three huge trees Jerry saw being who once described to himself as

"God!". Around him was intensive glow and it seemed that the light was everywhere. When approached this luminous man to Jerry about ten feet, he said the following: "Come here, son of the earth. You have a pure mind, and God help you. Your heart is now healed and will not bother you anymore. We want you to go home and then return to this mountain with your wife, and stay there for a month in June. At this time we will teach you both. There is no secret (mysticism), but a lot of truth and the truth will be revealed to you. Get ready for warm weather. "

Then, over time, Nola and Jerry arrived in June and stayed in the area of Mount Shasta, founding the campground. After one day holding hands and saying a prayer in thanks for healing Jerry, they suddenly saw a large rock moved and the land trembled. And there was a solemn voice:

"Beloved Children of the Earth, Power of God, which has no borders, has brought you here. I am the voice of the divine reality. We have invited you here to teach these laws to all the children of Earth to use them correctly and faithfully. There is nothing mystical. This is not a gift of a specific person. No one was elected, but only if he decides to serve truth and light. You have the time and if you gave permission, then by the will of God will send an angel to teach you and you will be able to help other people on earth.

We do not take anything from you, do not require you to any oath or promise. We ask that you establish your life and find time for this program, learn to think differently to see more clearly and understand. Divine laws are now working on the Earth as well as the time when Jesus Christ walked the earth.

I am Phylos, Tibetan, I was Zalim, the man from Atlantis. I am a high priest in the Great White Brotherhood Order of Melchizedek. My vote goes out of the Temple which is located in Mount Shasta. If you decide to meet us near the three trees, we'll teach you. "

I shall not go on to write, you can find yourself book and find out what happened next. But I will say that Nola has survived her husband. She received dictations of the Ascended Masters, are shorthand for many, many years. Nola has organized a school, and in general a lot of work to bring the message of knowledge to those who open their minds to.

Nola passed away in 1979.

Emily Frank, a news reporter Dunsmuir, shortly before the death of Nola Van Valer has interviewed her. Fully this unique interview can be found here:

http://www.mountshastamagazine.com/mystique/

In 1922, Jesus appeared physically before Nola Van Valer, she described it in her small book THE TRAMP AT MY DOOR.

And then, living in Mt.Shasta she for ten years, met directly with Jesus Christ who also taught her. I want to place here small fragment of that interview.

NV: Yes I met Jesus and he doesn't look like the pictures and paintings we've all seen. He's more than average height. He doesn't have long hair, nor a beard. He doesn't look anything like what we've been led to believe. He's light complected.

EF: You were quoted once as saying that a new Messiah is coming.

NV: There won't be a "new" Messiah. He will come anew. He will be here by the year 2000-could be before. A great change is taking place over the earth. By the year 2000 we won't be anything like we are now. A great change is coming. True religion will be in existence all over the world.

EF: What's going to happen then? Will everyone live in harmony? There will be no heaven or hell?

NV: There will be peace. It will be a new world. There is no hell-we make our own discomforts. That's a good name for it. . .

In the interview, there are things that I can not agree. For example, Nola said that in the Bible is written only the truth.. However the description of the future Messiah who is Jesus Christ, but has a different appearance, said to me personally that of Grigori Grabovoi came to this time from future and gave knowledge in order to prepare mankind to accept Teachings of the Eternal and Harmonious Development.

I understand that for some readers this is not evidence. But when I read these lines in an interview, you probably felt a sense that scientists feel when they do open or find proof of his theory. NOLA DESCRIBES APPEARANCE Grigori Grabovoi. MESSIAH came to her from the future and I see this as normal in accordance with the logic of the situation ... We live in the twenty-first century and to present the Messiah in the long robe and sandals, it is difficult for me personally. And this is putting it mildly.

Grigori Grabovoi came to Nola Van Valer in its present form.

CHAPTER 9

ORTHODOX RABBI DISCLOSES THE NAME OF THE MESSIAH

RABBI YITZCHAK KADURI

This story happened a few years ago, but I just now found out about it. Apparently it's the right time.

Rabbi Yitzhak Kaduri disclosed the name of the Messiah before he died; February 2006 somewhere between the age of 106 and 117, 300,000 attended his funeral in Jerusalem. He was a famous rabbi and cabbalist in the world, and knew the Torah perfectly. This man in his lifetime was regarded as wise and even holy, had a photographic memory, in his presence, people there were miraculously cured.

The Baghdad-born cabbalist had gained notoriety around the world for issuing apocalyptic warnings and for saying he personally met the long-awaited Jewish Messiah in November 2003.

Before Kaduri died, he reportedly wrote the name of the Messiah on a small note, requesting it remained sealed for one year after his death. The note revealed the name of the Messiah as "Yehoshua" or "Yeshua" - or the Hebrew name Jesus.

Death Note of Rabbi Yitzhak Kaduri
The name of Messiah
Yehoshua
Посмертная записка Рава Ицхака Кадури
Имя Мессии
Иехошуа

The note, written in Hebrew and signed in the rabbi's name, said: "Concerning the letter abbreviation of the Messiah's name, He will lift the people and prove that his word and law are valid. This I have signed in the month of mercy."

The Hebrew sentence consists of six words. The first letter of each of those words spells out the Hebrew name Yehoshua or Yeshua.

The finding has raised a combination of excitement and controversy in both Jewish and Christian circles - but scarcely any media attention. Jewish blogs and web forums are filled with skeptical analysis and puzzlement.

"So this means Rabbi Kaduri was a Christian?" asked one poster rhetorically.

Another wrote: "The Christians are dancing and celebrating."

Not exactly.

About his encounter with the Messiah Kaduri claimed he is alive in Israel today, he reportedly told close relatives: "He is not saying, 'I am the Messiah, give me the leadership.' Rather the nation is pushing him to lead them, after they find [in my words] signs showing that he has the status of Messiah."

"It is hard for many good people in society to understand the person of the Messiah," Kaduri wrote before his death. "The leadership and order of a Messiah of flesh and blood is hard to accept for many in the nation. As leader, the Messiah will not hold any office, but will be among the people and use the media to communicate. His reign will be pure and without personal or political desire. During his dominion, only righteousness and truth will reign."

Kaduri wrote that not all will believe in the Messiah - and that it will often be easier for non-religious people to accept him. He also describes a Messiah who is, at first, not aware of his position.

A few months before his death, Kaduri gave a Yom Kippur address in which he gave clues as to how to recognize the Messiah. He told those gathered for the Day of Atonement in his synagogue the Messiah would not come until former Prime Minister Ariel Sharon dies.

Sharon was stricken while in office Jan. 4, 2006. He remained in a coma until replaced by Prime Minister Ehud Olmert. While many expected the imminent passing of Sharon, he has remained alive but unconscious ever since his attack.

Shortly after what Kaduri characterized as his Nov. 4, 2003, encounter with the Messiah, in which he said he learned his name, the rabbi began warning of impending disasters worldwide.

In 1990, the late Lubavitcher Rebbe Menachem Schneerson told Kaduri that he would live to see the coming of the Messiah.

Also in September 2005, Kaduri said: "The Messiah is already in Israel. Whatever people are sure will not happen is liable to happen, and whatever we are certain will happen may disappoint us. But in the end, there will be peace throughout the world."

Ə Aviel Schneider, the author of the Israel Today story, said the worldwide reaction to news of Kaduri's note has been "crazy." He said he has never received so many emails and calls from around the globe.

He said he was urged not to publish the story by the rabbi's yeshiva, where officials said it was "impossible" that the note was actually written by Kaduri.

But Schneider was given access to many of the rabbi's manuscripts, written in his own hand for the exclusive use of his students. He was struck by symbols painted by Kaduri all over the pages.

"They were crosses," said Schneider. "In the Jewish tradition, you don't use crosses. You don't even use plus signs because they might be mistaken for crosses. But there they were, painted in his own hand."

From experience I know that the knowledge and vision of all the seers still interpret through the lens of his personality and ideas, so that the distortion may occur in the so-called "little things, in detail," but the main idea comes basically accurate.

Yitzhak Kaduri certainly knew that if he will publish in his lifetime that statement, then the consequences could be unimaginable just as Jesus Christ in the religious system of the Jews is quite an odious figure. Once in Moscow many years ago I found a synagogue when I went on a trip to the Middle Management Engineering and side by side there was the synagogue in which I went was to ascertain the attitude of a rabbi to Christ ... I just was curious. But after receiving the information soon safely crossed in the Church of Biysk in the Altai Mountains in Siberia, with my two daughters. I was told that Jesus was just a healer. Well, he walked among the people there, talked a lot to say very disputable things. Rabbi definitely did not like me and could hardly get rid of me, so strange women. I told him that I though thoroughbred Jew by birth and has a very religious forefathers in past generations. So that the assertion of Yitzhak Kaduri is a courageous and honest act. It is sensation! This is explosive information!

Ariel Sharon was an Israeli politician and general, who served as the 11th Prime Minister of Israel until he was incapacitated by a stroke on January 4, 2006 and died eight years later, on January 11, 2014. As far as I realized Grigori Grabovoi will soon appear in Israel and perhaps give the lectures about the transition of humanity to a state of immortality. Time has come.

I want to mention a very important point that if the rabbi physically communicated with the Messiah in Israel, it does not mean that the Savior is in this country right now. This example will prove the fact. Recently I received a call from New York. It was Tamara Hooke, an intelligent woman who had a degree and who devoted her life to the creation of inter-ethnic international language.. In conversation, she told me the following incident from her life. This took place February 17, 2005 in New York when she was in her apartment, reading the book by Vladimir Sudakov "Savior. The phenomenon of millennia Grigori Grabovoi." And suddenly against the window appeared screen red in color with black grille. A front of the grille a meter away from her in full height appeared Grigori Grabovoi in a light shirt, dark suit and tie. He spoke calmly and confidently, but the voice could be heard. There was no confusion. This vision lasted a minute...

One should consider that in 2005, nothing was yet known about the events that followed in 2006. Here I'm referring to his imprisonment. For her, as a scientist, inventor, and just a wise person, Grigori Grabovoi is the Messiah. Tamara Hooke is not a follower, she is on her own, but has acknowledged him in her soul and all her being! Tamara, like Yitzhak Kaduri could argue that Grigori Grabovoi was then in New York, but it may obviously not be proven.

these are the mysterious ways of the Lord, about how the Savior shows up on the Earth and in the hearts and minds of earthlings. We are talking of Divine Knowledge which He had brought for immediate rescue, salvation of the planet and the transition to a new quality: Eternal and Harmonious Development.

CHAPTER 10

EDGAR CAYCE ON THE "SECOND COMING"

Edgar Cayce (1877 – 1945) was an American psychic who allegedly had the ability to give answers to questions on subjects such as healing or Atlantis while in a hypnotic trance. Though Cayce himself was a devout Christian and lived before the emergence of the New Age Movement. Cayce has variously been referred to as a Sleeping Prophet, a "mystic", a "seer", and a "charlatan"

Cayce's methods involved lying down and entering into what appeared to be a hypnotic trance or sleep state, usually at the request of a subject who was seeking help with health or other personal problems The subject's questions would then be given to Cayce, and Cayce would proceed with a reading.

When out of the trance he entered to perform a reading, Cayce said he generally did not remember what he had said during the reading. The unconscious mind, according to Cayce, has access to information which the conscious mind does not — a common assumption about hypnosis in Cayce's time.

The Cayce readings had much to say about the life of Jesus—covering the "lost" years that were never addressed in the Bible. But Cayce also spoke of Jesus' return and here is an excerpt on that subject:

"Q. What is meant by 'The day of the Lord is near at hand?'

A. That as has been promised through the prophets and the sages of old, the time, and half time, has been and is being fulfilled in this day and generation... The Lord, then, will come, 'even as ye have seen Him go.'

Q. How soon?

A. When those who are His have made the way clear, passable, for Him to come."

(From Edgar Cayce Reading #5749-4)

"For He shall come as ye have seen Him go, in the body He occupied in Galilee. The body He formed, that was crucified on the cross, that appeared to Philip, that appeared to I, even John."
(Edgar Cayce Reading #5749-4, 8/6/33)

"Q. Are we entering the period of preparation for His coming?
"A. Entering the test period, rather.
"Q. When Jesus Christ comes the second time will He set up His Kingdom on earth, and will it be an everlasting Kingdom?
"A. Read His promises in that ye have written of His words, as John gave, 'He shall rule for a thousand years. Then shall Satan be loosed again for a season."
(Edgar Cayce Reading #5749-2, 6/28/32)

"Then, as to that second coming into the world--He will come again and receive His own, those who have prepared themselves through belief in Him and acting in that manner; for the Spirit is abroad, and the time draws near, and there will be the reckoning... He that hath eyes to see, let him see. He that hath ears to hear, let him hear that music of the coming of the Lord of this vineyard. And art THOU ready to give account of what thou hast done with thine opportunity in the earth as the Sons of God, as the heirs and joint heirs of glory with the Son? Then make thy paths straight, for there must come an answering for what thou hast done with thy Lord! He will not tarry; for having overcome, He will appear even as the Lord and Master. Not as one born, but as one that returneth to His own; for He will walk and talk with men of every clime, and those who are faithful and just in their reckoning shall be caught up with Him to rule and to do judgment for a thousand years."
(Edgar Cayce Reading #5749-7)

CHAPTER 11

GRIGORI GRABOVOI - WORLD TEACHER

> «He will walk among people and redistribute the wisdom of Almighty God.»
> (Jeane Dixon)

It is my deep conviction that such a man as the Savior of the World has the capacity/power of the Supreme Spirit manifested in childhood. Grigori Grabovoi has been manifesting his phenomenal abilities in front of many witnesses, as well as many strange and inexplicable events. Here is a fragment from the book by Elena Muhovikova, who met with the mother of Grigori Grabovoi Lyudmila Ilyinichna and *recorded the conversation.*

From the very infancy of Grigori himself had the awareness ofan adult/grown-up. He knew what he had come for on Earth, what goals and objectives were laying before him. He knew every language, understood the language of birds, animals, minerals, plants, and understood what they meant. Actually he could even hear such sounds as a waterfall a few miles away from his home. At the age of three years old the small Grigori already clearly saw the threat of destruction hovering over the Earth. The boy saw the human suffering, war, pestilence, destruction. But how could he help at this age? Hidden in a secluded place to avoid being disturbed, he thought, willed, placed the earth in his heart and an endless stream of love, released all tension from the planet, *without giving it a crack,* appeasing people. Already at three, small Grigori kept insisting that we must save the planet. His statements, extraordinary abilities and infinite knowledge and wisdom, tremendously astonished his relatives.

Lyudmila Ilyinichna tried to hide the abilities of her son from others, so as not to cause them a shock. She is very sorry now for such little time she had to talk to her unusual son. Lyudmila Ilyinichna worked 40 years as a chief accountant in the vehicle maintenance in the village.

"I had to work from morning to night to feed my family - she says, therefore Grigori was basically raised by my mother, with whom we had lived all our lives. Then she got Grigori baptised at age five. He was baptized by an old retired priest - a Greek, who was deported in Bogara from the city of Simferopol. "The name, unfortunately, I do not remember." Lyudmila Ilyinichna said that she had sent a report about the fact of the Immaculate Conception of her son together with his birth certificate to the church. But the birth certificate was never returned to her, so she had to order a new one. Grigori remembered the sacrament of baptism from other lifetimes, which allowed him to see the whole procedure in the higher plane in detail beforehand. Since then, an endless golden Ray of Light which is infinite relationship with God is inseparable from Grigori Grabovoi.

His grandmother was his greatest friend, whom he entrusted with all his secrets - says Ludmila Ilyinichna. She raised him as a true aristocrat. The grandmother's name was Klavdiya Kudrenkova - born out of an aristocratic family in 1893. Her father (great-grandfather of Grigori), Ivan Kudrenko was the king's officer, a land owner near Tashkent who grew cotton, and had a store in Tashkent that sold cotton abroad, up to the UK.

Grandmother was a very educated aristocrat. After the revolution, her father and brothers were *repressed* and arrested. Since then, she has never seen them. Once she left school, my mother sang in the Cathedral in the church choir. She knew the prayers, the Orthodox rituals and festivals that are celebrated at home." Told Lyudmila Ilyinichna, she was born in Sara – Agach, Kazakhstan. Her father (grandfather of Grigori) Bozhanov Ilya Ivanovich worked as chief engineer at a Machine and tractor station. Since 1945, the family was living in Bogara, Kazakhstan.

Grigori's father - Peter Grigoryevich Grabovoi eleven years older than his mother, was wounded in the war. Peter Grigoryevich worked on vehicle maintenance, he had a dream to connect Grigori to road work. Lyudmila Ilyinichna recalls that often in the evenings and into the nights Grigori and him had long conversations. "They always had something to talk about, but ... what? For me it remains a mystery" - complains Lyudmila Ilyinichna.

Grigori grew up a quiet boy who never raised his voice, no yelling, no fighting, and was completely healthy. According to his mother, he never had a medical history: he was never sick, received no vaccinations and never visited a doctor.

When Grigori was five years old, his parents decided to take him to an old muslim seer, Azeri, who lived in the village of "Ilichevka" - 20 km away. Lyudmila Ilyinichna says: "When we entered his yard, we were met by the clairvoyant's son. He began to say that his father did not accept to see anyone anymore as he was 80 years old and was very weak. We had turned around and wanted to leave, but we were stopped by heart-rending cries from the old seer, who demanded to bring the Russian boy to him immediately. "

the Parents were asked to stay with in the yard. Passed a long agonizing hour of waiting before Grigori reappeared. "Grisha, (nickname. Author's Note) what has he done with you that took so long?" - Said Lyudmila Ilyinichna. "Nothing" - Grigori said. "He fell to his knees in front of me and kissed first my hand, then my forehead, and then prayed for an hour." Then the old man stood up and again kissed my hands, forehead and told me to now invite you to him." When the parents were brought to the old seer, he solemnly asked them if they knew that their son was born of God?

Lyudmila Ilyinichna confirmed with a nod. The old man continued: "Your son is a God conceived child and not a hair should fall from his head. Protect him as the apple of your eye and do not expose him too much anymore. The boy has excellent health. If anyone dares to offend him, then he will lay down a curse on the seven tribes." Remembering the guidance from the old seer, his grandmother became Grigori's main guardian, who accompanied him everywhere.

At school, Grigori was elected as chairman of the class. He tried to educate classmates by example: he was always calm, never raised his voice at anyone. Healthy, with absolutely normal psyche, Grigori sat quietly at his desk, seemingly no different from others. But mentally he could save the world. In fifth grade, Grigori studied the workings of remote operation (also known as psycho or telekinesis).

Lyudmila Ilyinichna recounted how at Grisha's school, near the main entrance, there was a broken window pane with shabby paint, which was kind of spoiled and gave the building its sloppy appearance. Grigori often said to his classmate Tazhibayev Erken that it was necessary to install a new window pane. Grigori asked: "At least repaint it if you do not want it repaired." But none of the adults did listen to his repeated requests.

Then Grigori, for educational purposes, in full view of children, with a single and powerful glance, remotely knocked it off, the whole structure bent, while the nails went flying and got hooked on a tree. In order for the frame not to fall from the tree and not to traumatize children, *Grigori had managed to hit the top and break off the branch on which hung the frame.* After this, the staff of the school were forced to put a new window pane . But still Grigori's grandmother had to pay for it.

Grigori often advised adults, on when it was best to plant seeds in the garden, where best to plant a tree, predicted future events, often warned classmates of reckless behavior. And if they did not listen, then tried to divert them from trouble. *Grigori remembers how he once warned his classmate Aubakirova Asana is not going to boom, though it all went through it.

But the boy did not listen to Grigori, after school, he climbed up on the boom and fell.* At this time Grigori came out of school, and he had to make a strong mental control to save the boy. Grigori several times rescued people from drowning in the river and two *raised:* "I looked with the help of clairvoyance, to see who was drowning. I ran back to the river, jumped into the water and saved them. In some cases I have done extreme methods of Salvation "- he once confessed in conversation.

To his sister, Grigori described the appearance of her future groom and predicted the exact date she would get married.

Grigori's parents dreamed that he would attend University to become Automobile and Road Engineer. So, after graduating from high school he was sent to study at Ust-Kamenogorsk University in Kazakhstan.

Lyudmila Ilyinichna says that after the departure of her son she did not have any news: "We were very worried and began looking for him in Ust-Kamenogorsk, but he was not there." When she phoned her daughter in Tashkent, it turned out that Grigori had entered the Tashkent University. "Anyway, he went his own way, but not as we wished."

Then there were the brilliant studies at the Tashkent University in the Department of Applied Mathematics and Mechanics. Konstantin Rumyantsev testifies that as a student Grigori shocked students and teachers by giving instant answers to any problem. Grigori was not the least interested in intermediary calculations, "why bother with long and difficult processes to solve problems, if you already know everything?"- He explained.

Grigori loved going to the mountains and practicing karate.

Once during a school break,Grigori went to see his mother at work at the motor depot. He told her: "I will do so that the machine does not break, and not cause an accident." Grigori walked into the entire park of machines, and made some reality management. And in fact, stopped the machine from breaking. "During that year there was not a single accident "- says Lyudmila Ilyinichna.

She also recalled that once her sister's daughter, niece Olga, and her schoolmate from Samara came for the Summer holidays. At this time, Lyudmila Ilyinichna was gone from home for a month, leaving the care of the two girls to Grigori. He had then completed his first year in University and was home on vacation in Bogar. Grigori watched them spending their time aimlessly for two days; and then went and wrote them a schedule for the holidays. One day, Olga and her friend decided to go swimming in a canal. Grigori saw that directly into the collector there were chemicals that had emerged from a tractor. Floated on the surface of the water dead and poisoned fish. Swimming was therefore life threatening. Grigori tried to dissuade her, but Olga did not want to hear it. So to divert her attention, Grigori created the sighting of an airplane in the air, which hovered just in one place. This phenomenon was seen by people for half an hour in Bogar. Olga said this to Lyudmila Ilyinichna after her arrival. Lyudmila Ilyinichna, clasping her hands emotionally, replied: "Grisha, what are you doing? There are people.
"

During his second year at the University, Grigori began to investigate the causes of cancer and develop treatments for them. He gave many valuable and effective prescription of treatments for cancer patients to the Head of Pulmonology Cancer Institute in Tashkent - Svetlana Ikramova Abdullaevne. She was just shocked that Grigory P., possessed such knowledge in medicine, while studying at the Faculty of Applied Mathematics and Mechanics, she had originally taken him for an outstanding physician, yet in principle, he was not.

While in University Grigori Grabovoi did political discourse. He has performed with the protests against the senseless war in Afghanistan, which eventually got the attention from the *Secret Services. During his studies at the University Grigori often earned his living by preparing some *rationalization proposals* or calculation sheets for teachers. At the same time he studied the *target of control.* After graduation Grigori Grabovoi worked at the Secret Tashkent Design Bureau, where he developed new space and aviation technologies.

Instantly he could find the cause of the breakdown or failure of any aggregate, technical unit or device. Could detect violations of any of the technical processes and recommend the methods to eliminate them.

the abilities of the young professional drew the attention of the Civil aviation. He began to inspect the safety of aircrafts, including the presidential plane.

All psychic forecasts given by Grigori Grabovoi to his colleagues came true. In fact, they were confirmed to be one hundred percent accurate, which set a new precedent in the history of Uzbek Aviation, starting with the agreement of 02. 12. 1991 the contract between the number 9 SP "ASCON" and Uzbek Office of Civil Aviation (1992 - National airline of Uzbekistan). This agreement officially marked the beginning of a new trend in the diagnosis of aviation equipment, their processes, and the investigation, forecasting and prevention of accidents.

Chief of UzbekistanUGA Gani Rafikov Mazitovich testified: "I think all this new direction needs analysis and learning for the knowledge of such laws mastered by Grigori Grabovoi is not known to us, as it belongs to a hidden world. Knowledge of these laws may considerably shift many of our world views and paradigms of reality, will force humans to change their attitudes and many values, regardless of their age, nationality and religion. One thing I know for sure is that the knowledge possessed by Grigori Grabovoi opens new horizons for mankind in its understanding of the laws of the universe."

Further work has begun in Moscow, where Grigori Grabovoi moved following the invitation of Russian President Boris Yeltsin. Two months before a possible global catastrophe in Bulgaria, Grigori Grabovoi sent their Government a list of failures and remedies for the Kozloduy nuclear power plant, where some of the processes started to get out of control. A commission was established, which confirmed the entire list of failures. *Operatively, using the recommendations of Grigori Grabovoi, all problems have been eliminated. Physicists have proven that hazardous procedures in a nuclear reactor could cause an explosion. In the event of a crash, hot fusion plasma could rush to the center of the earth, leaving only dust on it. Thus was averted a global catastrophe, before which even the Chernobyl accident pales.

Another known fact is when Grabovoi was able to indicate the location for the trapped miners in Vorkuta mine, using remote viewing, having the only one scheme of the mine. In the same manner he has been preventing and avoiding many accidents in space.

In 1995, Grigori Grabovoi wanted to follow the whole curriculum of the Orthodox University. "I had to give up, because the church considered my abilities as a miracle. If we admit the divine status of all human beings, we can then conclude that everyone can learn this"- recalls he.

There was a time when was introduced to the Ministry of Emergency Situations for their efficient operations the patent number 214 845, Grabovoi's "method of preventing accidents and device for its implementation." Through digital processing carried out on technical devices, Polytron and CM (crystal module), with the use of mathematical methods for the numerical Runge-Kutta method, we can predict and mitigate the consequences of possible accidents, earthquakes, and protect people from terrorist attacks. Digital technologies developed modules (floppy digitalized and the digitalized label) *topical* application to prevent damage to buildings.

Grabovoi has developped mathematical analysis on global nuclear security, which was a point of his presidential program for 2008. All nuclear weapons, and eventually all weapons of mass destruction, will be taken very far into the orbits of remote systems.

In a difficult moment of his life Grigori Grabovoi wrote a small recollection of the memories of his childhood. And it was so unexpected and so unusual for him to do so because he is by nature rather a very private person .... We have the good fortune to know of some of these amazing and rare accounts, taken from his biography, written by his own hand.

"I was born in Kazakhstan, village of Bogara. Later the historians have established that it corresponds to the geographical location of Shambhala. From early childhood I remember how on one side of our yard, every day I performed some spiritual work. Earth in the eye of my spiritual vision *rolled down* and could break. Concentration of my mind and spirit could bring it back in place. These actions continued for a long time and were hard work. One winter day early in the year I fixed my spirit on Earth so that it has ceased to turn.

Three days later, on Christmas, my grandmother, who was deeply religious and who prayed every day to the image of Holy Mother asked me to come out of the gate. It was evening but I got out of the gate of the yard. I was approached by children and a very tall boy pointed his finger at me and said: "It is Jesus Christ." The other children immediately began to point fingers at me and kept saying, first one, then followed by others,louder and louder shouting , "You are Jesus Christ." Then they suddenly stopped shouting and went away. Returning home, I asked my grandmother who were these kids, because they had never before been seen in our village. Grandma paused and then said that they came from far to our home. At the earliest school age, I shared with one of my friends some knowledge about the future and he asked me to tell him about all I knew.

I remember that I began to describe a future where machines are not dangerous and do the will of man, if he only believes. Gradually a lot of kids gathered around me and I told them stories about the future of mankind. In Moscow, this friend came to my office and said that he remembered everything.

In 1979 I was on vacation with relatives at *vgorod* Samara. The pass was purchased for me so that I could go to this resort that was situated by the Volga River. There, I actually organized a daily sermon before a religious group on the topic of spiritual direction of technological development and application of Christian prayers for safety. The inhabitants of Samara are now actively involved in helping me.

In 1980 I organized a religious group in Uzbekistan, which has been studying mainly beneficial effects of the Christian commandment "Thou shall not kill" and prayers for the development of martial arts.

In 1988 I created a Christian religious group in Moscow with the main focus of sermons in the direction of eternal harmonious development of people.

In the early 90s I worked for the diagnosis of aircraft and Nora Raimovna Morozkina on Christmas Day told me that she saw me as the Second Coming of the Lord God Jesus Christ. Then she wrote the book "The Interpretation" which attested of this fact.

Diagnosis of aircraft carried me with Christian religious principles. The religious group has worked to spread knowledge of diagnostics equipment and eternal development of mankind.

In the 90's, evidence emerged claiming that I am the Second Coming of the Lord God Jesus Christ. Were then established many religious groups.

Representatives of fundamental religions always kindly greeted me. For example, the High priest of the Temple Qutab Minar Baba Nag Pal in India, who never made a mistake in his spiritual vision, told me that I was the second coming of the Lord God Jesus Christ.

Ministers of the Orthodox Christian Church also told me that I was the Second Coming of the Lord God Jesus Christ, proven by, among other things, my ability to accurately diagnose the equipment failures.

The priest of Saint Nina's, Father Gabriel, took me in Tbilisi during the ministry of the altar, and directed me to meet his parishioners. Many of the parishioners in a dream saw Orthodox saints come to them and told them that they were going to Grabovoi Grigori as he is the Second Coming of

Jesus Christ. there are evidences of this fact notarized by UNESCO.

Head of Education of the Moscow Patriarchate, the rector of religious education Father John wrote about me on the book "In God's help." Archbishop Orlovsky and Livenskij Master Paisios said to have written information about the meeting with me in the Golden Book of the Church. There have been many meetings with representatives of many religious faiths, and it has always been understood about the need to rescue people. "

I, Yelena Loginova, can write forever, but will stop in the hope that this information will help to wake up those who came under the spell of the false media, and find the strength and courage to further investigate the matter. We can not all be wrong... We are all on the same wavelength.

I had a friend that I had never seen, but we communicated for a long time. This pleasant and intelligent woman has worked with Grigori Grabovoi in Tashkent's closed Design Bureau. She is not a follower of the Doctrine and not a member of any party or any religious movement, but says Grigori Grabovoi is someone perfect, very special, strong and loving. She is a physicist and mathematician, and not for a moment doubted that Grigori Grabovoi is the one who was awaited for ages. Hearing from this woman, who for many years personally knew him and his family, is extremely valuable.

"You ask: how is he as a person? Well in fact, it may be different for everyone. But if you are interested in my personal and honest opinion, I can say that he's the most honest, intelligent, sympathetic, clever ..... I can continue indefinitely - I'm in a loss for words. Here I am very tormented by your next question: Is he the Second Coming? I have to admit, when you know the person for a long time, consider him a friend, you talk with him freely on any topic, and in such mundane conditions, it is somehow frightening to imagine that you could live nearby someone who'd turn out to be such a person. Honestly, I do not consider myself a student of his, neither do I spread the teachings in the sense in which it is done by his disciples. But I still took from all that he gave to people. For me, from the very beginning, there seemed to be some instances of miracles, but then I clearly understood that this was all from God, and God does all this without any of our notion of miracle. So many people, after recovering, will ask some silly questions: like was I sick at all? Again, God puts each person in front of a choice: either to believe or not. Different cases were major ones, but since I did not focus attention on the miracle, my memory was clearing them away to make room for vital information.

I never saw him angry and frightened. He could go into a fight with any number of people. He studied karate. A very hardy and very secretive man. Absolutely fearless. What's going on inside him we'll never understand. In public he is always cheerful, willing, but never shows if something is wrong with him. It is amazing how he had so much power. "

I also got acquainted with Elena Egereva who is a wife of Grigori Grabovoi. And for me, that she's into a loving relationship with such an extraordinary husband is also evidence. After all, everyone knows that those who have the most difficulty to perceive the genius are family members... Some day a talented writer will write a book for her courage and selfless work. Elena is very feminine and reminds *Decembrist that the most difficult years did not betray their husbands.*

I sincerely admire the Russian woman, a mother and wife of a great man.

I have the day off, but I sit and write serious stuff. I look at myself as an outsider, and laughed ... The little woman has settled into a chair, cross-legged before the computer, the tail on the side, her hair carelessly combed. She wears soft fleece pants, has a drawing with colored cats... A thought flashed in my head that I should have time to cook, to buy food, feed the cat and walk the dog.

But I know how deceiving it can be... After all, if fate gave me the "accidental" meeting in Moscow, on the street, with Grigori Grabovoi immediately the next morning after my arrival in Russia; if in India, at the home of Helena Roerich (Kullu Valley), I had the privilege of sitting in an armchair, where she received the message and Teaching of Agni Yoga, from the Great Masters of Shamballa; was in the residence of the Dalai Lama and drinking tea with his sister. If I saw and heard many times the great Indian saint Sai Baba; had a private letter to my home address from Senator Edward Kennedy; and if by chance into our house got odious Vladimir Zhirinovsky; and Bill Clinton responded personally to the letter my youngest daughter sent him in 1999. And Hillary Clinton at one moment suddenly appeared side by side at me and there is a picture ... If I had a personal encounter with the first millionaire Artem Tarasov, Russia; if my friend is the great doctor of the world Chechen Hassan Baiev and also another friend, historian Vladimir Malsagov; if a minute after my email Uri Geller answered personally ... a lot more - so it's not by chance but for a reason and purpose. I am writing so much with only one sole purpose: to cause your trust to my words, so that you too have realized - the Second Coming of Jesus Christ on earth had happened. Help yourself and us all together to avoid macro-catastrophe and to step into Eternity.

CHAPTER 12

Nora Raimovna Morozkina about Grigori Grabovoi

Nora Raimovna Morozkin is one of the most active followers of the Teaching of Grigori Grabovoi. And sometime as far as in 1991 she already had a senior management position in a major Aviation Company in which, after graduation, she got a job in KB (design bureau) where Grigori grabovoi started working as a first job. Until 1998 she worked as Director of Information and Computing Center of the national airline of Uzbekistan. Nora Raimovna Morozkin has been working with Grigori Grabovoi since 1991, has been closely involved in all the papers and experiments that GP held at the National Aviation Company.

In her book, Nora Raimovna very sincerely, humanly and warmly writes about getting acquainted with a young graduate, and what has then resulted. I will give a very significant piece of this exclusive book yet, but you judge for yourself...

"My Search of the Knowledge of the interactions of the laws of the universe brought me to a group of extraordinary people who enthusiastically studied the esoteric literature. In this circle, which met on the basis of common interests, there were a few psychics. I continued to work in the Aviation company. Nobody knew about my diagnosis, it suits me. On duty, I had to attend to parse disasters airlinerstaking place in our country and in other offices of Aeroflot. It's a shame to hear that the cause of accidents most often was "human factor". But what can I do? Perhaps using the gift of clairvoyance, psychics have been able to diagnose the basic life-support systems of aircraft before their takeoff! Science Fiction? But what if we try to bring my new friends? I asked this question at the next meeting. There were various proposals. I outlined the conditions under which I take upon myself the responsibility to come up with the proposal to the leadership of Airline: All experiments should be conducted in a production environment, in compliance with the purity of the experiments and recording results.

Of the seven present at this discussion of psychics to work on such harsh conditions agreed to only one - Grigori Grabovoi. Over the shoulders of this young man, a graduate of the Tashkent State University has been the practice of using his clairvoyance in the design office for space issues, where he worked after graduation. I knew that we would be pioneers in this matter, but intuitively I was sure of the correctness of this path. All work on the development of the experimental conditions was carried out in the evenings after work, when we were all relieved of our duties. Within two - three weeks have been identified forms of requests, responses, acts, protocols. Grigori conquered all of us, with his simplicity and accessibility. He managed to respond to a variety of questions quickly and easily. Although this seeming ease was the exact knowledge of the laws of the Universe to the extent that he, almost casually gave information about unfamiliar people, events, facts, know in advance about which he could not. For example, the control question Radik software engineer about his sister and her health (the sister was at this point in Ufa), Grigori gave him the information in such detail about that in our circle no one could know. Somewhat later, Radik, at my request, the information recorded on paper, confirming the full accuracy of the information received from Grigori as the state of health of his sister, and events. This document is stored in our archives to this day.

My unusual proposal for carrying out experiments on the use of clairvoyance of Grabovoi in the diagnosis of aircraft to improve safety, I presented my case rather emotionally. The General Director listened to me without interrupting. By the end of my tirade for the glory of clairvoyance, I saw in surprise raised eyebrows and heard from General Director the following words: "It's fantastic, even if I believed you, then I do not understand in government circles. Also, I do not have the right to officially use such methods ". To which I enthusiastically replied: "If you can prevent a disaster at least one aircraft with the help of this method, the game should start." The General Director was silent thoughtfully. The pause lasted long. I broke down and spoke again: "At one time in the Soviet Union was announced the pseudo-science of cybernetics, which came out of it I did not tell you.

I think that in the developed world have investigated the ability of such people in enclosed areas of science and technology. This was not written in books and scientific journals, but very soon this issue will cease to be the property of only fantastic stories. "He looked at me like a hurt child, feeling that I wholeheartedly believed in every word. Then, fatherly encouragingly said, "Okay, persuaded, bring your clairvoyant, let's see what he can do." I "flew" out of the office of General, as if on wings. I called Grigori. Announced the appointment of the meeting. It took everything for not showing too much emotion, as if I met with the ministers every day. It seemed that he knew in advance the outcome of negotiations. Two days later, Grigori and I went at the appointed hour in the Office of the Director Airline of Uzbekistan. He looked at Grigori, and almost immediately asked: "Can you really look into the past and the future?" Calmly and quietly sounded the answer from Grigori: "I can." Their eyes met and they are keenly looking at each other for several seconds. General then said, "Then try to describe the catastrophe of our aircraft in Kabul, Afganistan" Grigori asked to report the date of the event and tail number of aircraft. I have carefully looked at him. A short pause. He apparently has not changed, only trembled eyelashes, and eyes were detached. In seconds, he looked at pieces of the event and with a muffled voice began his tale: "I see a man striding confidently along a mountain trail with an extended backpack. Here he stopped. Began located. Prepare a place for lying down. Untied the bag and pulled out of the weapons with telescopic sights.

"Now look at what a system." Again, a short pause, then very clearly Grigori dictated the main characteristics of the system and described its features. We listened attentively and marveled at the clarity and consistency of its information. And he, without stopping for a second continued his story: "The point has been chosen in advance. From this place perfectly visible airspace before landing strip at Kabul airport.

Without changing the position and tone, Grigori suddenly said - the commission's decision was wrong, the plane was shot down. The crew is to blame. "I glanced at the General, and saw how hard his eyes narrowed. He knew that sitting in front of him a young man could not have information on the findings of the commission on catastrophe.

About which knew only a narrow circle of specialists, and the investigation materials were stored in strict secrecy. Confidence of young man alarmed the General. Grigori calmly continued: "The man in the ambush had to spend at least five or six hours, as the fighter planes are not on schedule. So he pricked up his ears and fell to the optical sight. The plane came in sight. The crew confidently displays it on the landing. The plane is visible in the optical sight. A shot. Projectile flashed trim the aircraft with a little clap. "

Grigori broke the story and looked questioningly at the General: "Continue?" General nodded in agreement. Grigori continued his steady voice description of what he saw: "The sound of a shell, breaking the body aircraft, heard only one watching the landing of the plane soldiers. He is one of a group of military guarding the airfield. But he said nothing about it, felt that it is not essential, because there was no explosion that could be seen. Visually, the explosion is not visible, but the projectile in excess of the thermal action, burst into the cabin, burned it all alive and not alive, too.

A short pause. His voice suddenly sounded surprising, and Grigori continued: "The left pilot still alive at the time of the explosion, he sat leaning back in his chair, and it served as a protective shield for the brain. When he awoke from the shock, he tried to fulfill his duty attempting his burned hands to land the plane. He pulls the wheel itself. The plane is subject to, its movement changed, but the consciousness of pilot is *extinguished and so a few attempts before life flickered out of him. By its action plane, fading to a sine wave lasted up to the airfield and crashed near the runway. "General, after a few seconds pause, which made Grigory frankly admitted to him: "You have confirmed my doubts. From the very beginning of the investigation I was convinced of the innocence of the most experienced crew. It is impossible in such conditions, an experienced crew to destroy themselves and technique. And probably most importantly, families and children perished in the war pilots were not only without them, but without benefits. This "worm" burdened my heart for a year. But your information as long as I can not be used as a rigorous proof. It is unfortunate that clairvoyance does not have legal status in this country. My intuition tells me that you're right. " General extended his hand to the panel with buttons to call the experts. He immediately replied a male voice: "Department of Safety, Inspector N listens." "Head of the helicopters came to me," - said the General. A minute later the chief inspector security helicopters appeared in the doorway. It was a man in uniform flying clothes, forty, strongly built and with a military bearing. He asked softly: The General invited him to the table and immediately without further clarification, asked to tell about what he knew about new anti helicopter engines? I am aware of the responsibility of the moment with bated breath waiting for his information. Amazingly, he started his presentation with a description of systems of shells over the thermal action. Then, almost word for word repeated performance of this system, we have heard from Grigori a few minutes ago. General thanked the inspector for the information and released him almost immediately. He had a lot to think about. This information is not possible to guess ... " General eyes surveyed the table. His gaze settled on the list of participants of the international meeting in London, where he planned to address the issue of acquisition of new aircraft. He handed a list to Grigori with the words: "I am flying to London to choose airlines Boeing or AS 10. Who among them can I trust? They are all persons interested in selling equipment. "Once again we had a surprise. Grigori, without having any information except that which was filed on his sheet of paper, and even in English, said confidently: "They all have a past meetings treat you well. But, in a particularly warm and honest relationship you can expect from Mr. K. He is a descendant of Russian immigrants, and feels for you the respect, as a representative of the homeland of his ancestors and as an outstanding personality, after your meeting with him at previous meetings on the same subject. "The General seemed to be unmoved and listened to Grigori as if every day he met with clairvoyants, but he broke down and stopped: "How do you know about our meetings?" His answer was given casually: "So it's all written in the field of information hidden agenda, and entering it is simple enough if you know the algorithm input. I know it. "Then, almost without a pause, he continued: "Among the participants in your meeting the most colorful figure is N. He mulatto, with short hair curly, graying hair, about fifty years old. He *pin* and sociable person, the soul of companies.*

Interestingly, he does not smoke or drink. Now let's see why? "And in a moment, confidently said:" Clearly, the residual hematoma in the head after a car accident. It provokes strong migraine pain after taking alcohol or nicotine. But this does not prevent him to be happy and cheerful person without these supplements doping. "

The General knew that Grigori was - an unusual phenomenon, but a decision on the introduction of unique experiments on a contractual basis, were not immediately resolved. "My position requires me to attach to the contract specific materials confirming your ability to diagnose equipment in such an unusual way - he said, referring to Grigori,

"I will allow you to work at the airport for a month with the engineering staff of aviation and technical base. If by December you put me on the table the documents signed by our experts and confirming the accuracy of your predictions, I am ready to conclude an agreement. "He paused and looked inquiringly at Grigori. Grigori, nodding his head in agreement, said: "The materials we have obtained, prior to the month of December will be included in the accounting documents of the contract, since there will be a scientific interest." As a result, the contract was signed. All materials and documents on this case can be found in three volumes "The Practice of Management. The way of salvation."

The National Airline of Uzbekistan Grigori Grabovoi spent more than 300 hard experiments. We conducted experiments at the airport right in front of aircraft for flight-testing stations. Test pilots, aviation managers of enterprises have participated in these experiments. They are witnesses. We conducted the test in an aircraft factory shops, and everywhere we considered these as miracles for us. But for Grabovoi it is the ordinary work, because he has this great gift, and he teaches it to others.

In 1996 on the program "Third Eye" director of the program asked Grigori Grabovoi the question: "Excuse me, why do you never write, who are you? Psychic? Psychologist? "He simply said: "I do not ever write, who I am, so that no one was separated. The goal that I set myself - is the salvation of every person. "

In one of his lectures Grigori Grabovoi said: "We are faced with the task of unification and integration of all the people of planet Earth. If we do not change the consciousness of humanity, the possibility of global catastrophe is inevitable. It has already been prepared by our civilization currently"

One correspondent of a Russian newspaper asked NK Morozkina:»How do you comment on that statement, GP Grabovoi that he was Jesus Christ, the Second Coming?"

N.R.Morozkina: When Grigori Grabovoi announced that he is the Second Coming of Jesus Christ, for many it was like a shock therapy. This can give a name for how people reacted to it. For us who have worked for many years with Grigori Petrovitch, it was just a consequence. Why not? Because come close to the Teaching those people who are engaged in spiritual practices until then. If we read the well-known visionaries, people who valued civilization, is what they say about the future? We will see the forefinger on the fact that this should happen around 2000.

The Gospel speaks metaphorically about everything, but if any of you read The Aquarian Gospel, written by a priest from Ohio (America), there is very specific information about this fact, saying that the Son of Man will appear in the East, will show his capabilities, will give the world new science, that will allow people to expand their consciousness. If we honor the Koran, there clearly is stated as follows: "And the angel said to Mary, that thou shalt have a son, and he will be glorified in the near and the last World." What is the last World? The Gospel speaks of the end of the World, What is the end of the world? This is the beginning of a new Light. Again the interpretation is such that it must be understood. The Gospel points out that at the heart of the Christian faith is the resurrection of Christ. Two thousand years before Christ showed that the resurrection is possible, and also the disciples, the apostles, addressed these issues. In the Gospel it is written: "You recognize me on the fact that I will do."

That's it going. Grigori Petrovich said at one of his lectures on religion: "Faith can not be embedded in the human, faith comes through practice. The man, realizing the Teachings and advice that I give, and receiving the results of using the Technologies of Consciousness, of course, understand that this divine knowledge, which I handed to him. "Long-suffering people can not take for granted that knowledge. He shall build a new science, which will be the science and practice. It will show people that this is true. And it is by creating his science, he can rebuild the world. "

Corr.: Why, then, the Orthodox Church does not recognize Grabovoi as Christ?

NR Morozkina: I think, to make conclusions, then perhaps the church should not isolate itself from this, but find an opportunity to explore what is happening. I have a book of the Moscow Diocese, "Will we be able to recognize relatives and friends on the day of resurrection of the dead?" And it is endorsed by the Diocese. I'm not a dogmatist. I read the Gospel with a pencil in my hand. As a mathematician, physicist, as I have underlined that, on what I can lean the same way as in the Koran.

This set of laws and rules of human behavior on Earth. That's a position we like, we can look at it, it's great, and specifically states: "Love, respect, do good, do not steal, Thou shalt not kill, respect others' faith." The Koran also states: "Respect other people's faith." So I want to say, the priest Krotov published an article which says that if you criticize Grigori Grabovoi for the resurrection, then scold me, the Pope, etc., all those who, in principle, to know what lies at the heart of Orthodoxy resurrection. But the resurrection does not mean "bringing back the dead" - it is a technology that was known to civilization long ago, but was available only to initiates. Remember Pythagoras and his school, read. After all, they took only the elect. Not only that, they took an oath that the disclosure of knowledge that they would get there, would be punishable by death. Then mankind was not ready to accept this knowledge. That's how tough the conditions were set. Now, Grigori Grabovoi brings this knowledge and says: "The situation on the planet has developed in such a way that if we do not change the consciousness of humanity, then ..." People do not realize that by their of the consciousness, they dig a hole for themselves. We need to understand the situation. Our aggression, it is constantly forming in the future, a situation that we still have to overcome. And, in general, then it is unclear what is orthodoxy or Christianity. You see, Gregory P. says: "If we analyze the behavior of the priests, who say that the resurrection can not be, they behave as they do not know the foundation upon which all Christianity is built." Is not that so? Among the scientists they are the same.

CHAPTER 13

PRONOUNCING

June 5, 2004 in Moscow, Grigori Grabovoi held a press conference in which he stated that he is Jesus Christ in the Second Coming. Please understand correctly: the soul of Jesus and the soul of Grigori Grabovoi are one and the same. It is the same person.

"I Grabovoi Grigori Petrovitch, born November 14, 1963 in the village of Kirov, the village Bogara Kirov district of Shymkent region, Kazakhstan, declare that I am Grigori Grabovoi - The Second Coming of Jesus Christ. This statement I make on the basis of God's Word and the Word of God, and on the basis of what I am personally confident this was always, I mean, I always knew it was initially, from birth. And in this connection the statement - for me it is sufficient in this regard as simple as the statement is conducive for people to take action to save, by unanimous act of Salvation, when people, knowing this knowledge that I am the Second Coming of the Lord God Jesus Christ, - They can be saved by learning the knowledge that I give - Knowledge of my Teaching, and thus can pass the Good News all at once."

CHAPTER 14

THE UNEXPECTED VISION

I experienced one particular incident in my life in the end of the nineties, after which I took off a cross with a crucifix and carry a simple with a stone in the center... My seven year old daughter went to a very well known music group "Rainbow," in our town where she sang and performed on stage. One day, quite unexpectedly, came to me of her head, the director of musical group, Lyubov Gibodiev, and said that the first time in her life had a vision. She told me in detail what she saw, and I wrote down to remember.

I want to note that this strong and talented woman was very far from religion and everything connected with it. Anyway, at that time.

She told me the following:

"One day I asked God the question," Why would You, if You exist, make so to get around not such a mess? In fact, people can live better and could become more kind. "After that came unexpectedly the following vision: Before Lyubov Gibodeev suddenly appeared Our Lady, Mother of Jesus dressed in white. She remembered a very sweet face, femininity. The eyes of Lyubov Gibodeeva filled with tears when she told of this vision.

Virgin said: "People make a fatal mistake, they pray on my Son who was crucified. I find it very painful. After all, I bitterly mourned by his side, when my son was hanging on the cross. You insulted me with that for two thousand years. You should pray to the Lucky Star that appeared when He came into the world. And for that reason too you can see there and everywhere on the earth filled with all those suffering. People then did not understand much and then distorted the message. Prayers should be sent to our One. To our Creator. Thus in order to correct this distortion was sent Mohammed. In the Muslim religion there is almost no attributes, but God for us all is One. "It was also stated that now come to Century of Virgin and that wearing a cross on the chest with the crucified Jesus Christ is not to be done anymore. After these words through a beautiful face of the Virgin flowed tears.

I have before me a piece of calendar on which I wrote in small letters about the vision. It is the date of February 16, 1997. Sunday.

After all, Lyubov Gibodeeva this respected in city woman came to me to tell this. For some reason it is special. I think Mother of Jesus knew exactly the time that I have to protect her son, who now dare to be judged in Russia. He came under the name Grigori.

CHAPTER 15

RAMTHA ABOUT YESHUA BEN JOSEPH

There was such a moment. At the time, when I been corresponding with a woman who worked with Grigori Grabovoi in aviation design bureau when he was very young man, just after graduation. He told sometimes during the breaks to colleagues very surprising things, and everyone who was around was listening to him attentively and with interest. This woman is very sorry for not having written down what was said. But she told me the following: Grigori spoke calmly and without emotion, as something ordinary that Jesus was not a simple carpenter, but carried a royal blood, had an army ... However, she well remembered the following sentence: "Jesus had a family, three sons"

I find this information correct, because more and more historical documents began to appear just proving that Jesus had the wife and children. And a lot more different and distinct from conventional myths.

I really like Ramtha who speaks through JZ Knight since 1977. Those who have read the White Book of Ramtha would never say that such an immortal being does not exist. He is 35,000 years after his moment of ascension. But I will not dwell on it; I'll provide a few quotes from what said this remarkable ascended Master.

"Here was an entity who put aside the woman that he loved, his children, the throne, and had a message. Everyone can be the sons and daughters of their parents, but very few ever finally decide to say I am the royal blood of my Holy Spirit and this is the life that I must live.' "
— Ramtha

Yeshua ben Joseph had a wife. He knew what it was to make love to a woman and he knew what it was to have children. Did that cease his message? His message was enriched.
Don't you think he understood people? Yes. So what did he do that was

different than you? What are we talking about here?

This is what he did. The greatest teaching that was ever taught was the teaching on the mount

The difference between you and Yeshua ben Joseph is that Yeshua ben Joseph knew that he was born to be God, and so his life was dedicated to being the son of God even though he was born of a man. And when he was weak, he acknowledged, "It is my humanity; it is not the Father within me. The Father within me is the all-wise, knowing intelligence."

Why am I writing this? Because when people are becoming interested in the personal life of Teacher, then in some of them appears an internal conflict. But we must be very wise to understand that the Son of man is inherent in all that is human. And I like it!

CHAPTER 16

THE FALSE MESSIAHS

Over the past two thousand years many people have claimed to be the Second Coming. Only for the last hundred years I think with such a statement came minimum twenty men in the world. For example Indian Sai Baba. I like him, I was twice in Puttaparthi, where this amazing man has organized a wonderful ashram and the city itself looks like a fabulous, clean and comfortable one. But Sai Baba is not the Second Coming. He made a mistake, it is my firm conviction.

Let me give an example of two others, who claim that they are returned Jesus Christ. They are Vissarion and Sun Myung Moon -Korean Messiah

VISSARION

Vissarion - a person worthy of deep analysis and sober view of the situation. He, too, - is an extraordinary person. At first glance, his teaching is carrying light. But when you listen to Vissarion with anb independent and positively minded investigative look, the picture opens up with a quite

controversial aspect. People who had gathered in the community under Minusinsk in Siberia in the early nineties, probably for the most part are very open, good and hardworking people.

But here, I saw significant scope and limitations of ... "Few.Very few. Absolutely not ... "- loudly proclaims my soul. Vissarion's speeches for me are more restrictive bondage. Independent thinking is not welcome in the community and hierarchy prevails. It is a matter of taste of course, but a statement of Vissarion of him being the Messiah and the World Teacher for me just sounds inappropriate. I find it to be a case worthy of studying, but no more. Slave-psychology is not the best way to development. The idea of eternity in the ranks of the followers of Vissarion finds no sounding ear. But clearly heard the slogan to be fruitful and multiply, as well as some national aspects. But I had time to make friends with the not young lady, a poet who lives in New York: she had lived many years in the community of Vissarion and sent me some tapes of his speeches her deeply respected teacher... In this lovely woman there is not a feeling of any aggression, which I sometimes perceive in representatives of, say, and orthodox Catholics and Orthodox Christians. Also, to my surprise was adjusted warm relationship with Vadim Redkin, which, in my opinion, is the right hand of his teacher Vissarion. Vadim is amazing in his tolerance, has so much wisdom and I do not want to make anyone hurt. Aristotle said: "Plato is my friend, but truth is more expensive"

So I'll excerpt from an exclusive interview with physicist and bold researcher of the unknown with Y.I. Yaklichkin. I'll just leave the interview as it is, only you have to read up to the end and then it will be understood, by using some common sense. The world is diverse and we must cultivate a sense of discernment to be able to make the right choice. Sometimes parting with illusions is very painful...

"In November 1989 the club was formed called the" hypothesis "in Minusinsk, which began its work by studying the geopathic zones in the region of Perm, in the Eastern Sayan Mountains and in Khakassia. Headed this Sayan branch of the Siberian Scientific-Research Institute of Research on anomalous phenomena by Yuriy Yaklichkin.

- Yuri Ivanovich, the existence of your institution is simply fantastic. Its creation was indeed supported by the government?

- Not really. The idea of creating this first research center was approved only by the military. Probably because by the time they have studied the UFO landing, poltergeist phenomena, etc.

- The military did have a meeting with a UFO?

- Of course. The materials were kept secret, but some of them I've seen. Was Zaorshan landing object and aliens in Uzbekistan.There was a landing, takeoff, an encounter with aliens. I have seen samples of organic material, which is under the influence of the UFO turned to stone.

- And here in Siberia has there been meeting with extraterrestrials?

- There was a contact in Sosnovoborsk. There lived a certain man named Zhigachev, who in his body appeared large quantities of mercury after the meeting

— We watched him for four years, studied the mercury, its composition, in some parts of the body it occurs.

— To talk about this in our newspaper biophysicist Nicholas Grid.

— He, along with my son, who is now in Moscow doing dissertation on the genetics, studying mercury and cellular structures, which were seized during the operation.

— Where does the body was taken in the mercury?

— There was cold fusion.

— The body itself is synthesized mercury!?

— Do not body. We assume that in the synthesis of this material involved the basic structure. Let's go back to the binary organization of man. In humans, there are structures that govern its biological part. We concluded that the brain did not process information. Its main objective - getting information from a huge number of sensors and transfer it to the base unit - neurocomputer was built from neurons. From there, the brain receives the information. The base portion has a huge potential and can lead even the synthesis of a complex element of the periodic table as mercury. Literally two days after contact with Zhigachev were formed large lumps on his right leg and left arm. He appealed to the doctors. What surprise surgeons during surgery when the incision of the spilled mercury. The first time was extracted more than 200 ml of mercury. Over the years, Mercury has taken a considerable area. In total he made 12 major surgeries and 22 minor ones. We buried Zhigacheva in 1995. But he died not from mercury. Someone told him that alcohol is good to excrete mercury, well he tried. Yes, and he got carried away so that we did not have time to get him out binge. Besides, he used a low-quality alcohol.

(Here, I'll take off some of the details. Author's Note)

— Tell me, have you met with Vissarion at Minusinsk? He, too, with someone contacts.

— Vissarion (Sergei Torop) with his friend Vladimir Plesinym were members of our club in 1990. In the total mass of the 100 people he does not stand out. We had just tried to get in touch with other worlds. Then we were not clear with whom contact person. Some said that the gods, others - with the aliens. We needed to establish a physical basis, which is based contact, what its nature is and whether each person may be contacted. Raised a number of experiments and in one of them came into contact Plesin. If a person comes into contact, then writes a report, as it happens, what he sees how the emission. In general, information on the merits of this contact we have received. But then we noticed a strange thing: as soon as Plesin came into contact, he was immediately changed. He began to get to open the contact information on some of the new religion, which focused on space. He eventually broke away from us. We planned to study the psychic abilities of a person in terms of knowledge management biochemical processes in the body and sent people including Plesin in Moscow. And when three months later he returned, it was a different person. Plesin received information, but he tried not to show it. He walked away from us, carefully concealed his religious orientation. But I, as a leader, he brought me up to date. I am closely acquainted with Sergei Toropov, when they invited me to see his gallery of portraits. Subjects had a strange, grim picture. Then they were clearly focused where to go. It turned out they were trained in Moscow, at the Institute of Halperin's to new methods of human exposure.

- When I went to the Community of Vissarion, they told me that there is some special zone. There really is an anomaly?

- Frankly speaking, the anomalous zones is essentially non-existent. All of them are modeled artificially created and well supported.

- Who created? Lord God?

- An interesting question. In our studies of anomalous zones, poltergeist and contact forms, we found that contact is not with the gods, not with other civilizations, and with other life forms that have a globular structure. They recorded the video and film. Sometimes it can be seen even visually. This life form is a completely different matter, according to their physical properties unknown to us. They are well aware of our physical organization, a device that may enter the mind and program it. By the way, zombies - it's just a product of these creatures. They are free to rearrange the structure of human thinking and even ... to kill. Askizsky poltergeist, which we have studied for two years, killing three people. So, these life forms are involved in the creation of anomalous zones, which in some of their parts resemble poltergeist zone: changing the physical fields, the situation and made an impact on the person. And quite serious.

- It turns out that Vissarion came into contact, got the command and became according to the plan of globular structures to build the City of the Sun?

- Exactly

- That is, he does not act on his own program?

- Of course. These structures affect the the social consciousness of man, by organizing the sect and thus solve their own problems. But the actions of Vissarion, there are also an ordinary self-interest. Of a new religion, he gets an advantage for himself. He was there for them God authority, it's nice. But he also knows who works with him. He was at our center and has this information. In his sermons is a powerful effect on people.

- These spherical structures create a certain effect on the informational "neurocomputer" of person, changing not only his physical condition, but also thinking.

- And what psychiatrists think about contactees?

- Psychiatrists know only the physical basis of the disease. When we studied the contacts, and then went to the psychiatric clinic. There is 80% of the contactees. They can not be cured, because everything is at second base structure that is inaccessible to us because it is in a different space. Thanks to the binary, our Creator has achieved high accuracy of copying. Man lives and many thousands of years does not change its appearance from generation to generation. Therefore affect the structure medications is just silly. "

And yet, I think that Vissarion does good business, but I certainly do not think it is the Second Coming of Jesus Christ, as he claims. I have this right, however, as Vissarion has the right to assert the opposite.

Here is an excerpt from personal correspondence with Vadim Redkin, I think there is nothing that might offend, but shows the kind of face:

"Yes, it is natural. Anyone who appreciates any event through the prism of their own sensory world that is changing in some aspect in life. Man will never see the world objectively, like representatives of other sentient worlds of the universe. That's the fun. In this poetic individuality of man. Twelve years ago we were in Putaparti, India. I remember that time at the conference Avatar Sathya Sai told someone that he came and the land of Israel two thousand years ago. It is unlikely that so he could give you a direct confirmation as to the fact that Grabovoi is The Second Coming. Where a person chooses to tune with their world, there for him and Coming. For example, for me is the essence of Vissarion. But this is not ground for theological disputes. We, more importantly, learn to selflessly, without expecting anything in return, to love each other. Who will do it, he is always right. "

I answered to Vadim as follows: "I know that the main idea of the Vissarion community is: "the whole world will perish, but we will survive and become the beginning of a new humanity". Selfishness. Meanness.

Of course, love is a basic condition. But do get rid of mind control and become a Man in which are activated all the potentials inherent by our Creator and be able to model your own beautiful reality, to forget the very disgusting concept of aging, illness and death, is not a Goal? I'm talking about the transition of mankind to Eternal and Harmonious Development."

Sun Myung Moon - Korean Messiah

Now take a closer look at Mr. Moon. At the root of the "Movement association" which is now highly branched structure, established in many countries, is the San Myung Moon, who was born in the Korean peasant family in 1920, He spent his childhood in a family of followers of Korean shamanism based on Confucianism, and only in adolescence age-moon met with Christianity, when his family moved into one of the Protestant areas. The central ideological and organizational backbone of the movement is the "Unification Church", established in 1954 under the official name "Holy Spirit Association for the Association of World Christianity." According to supporters of the Mr. Moon, the future prophet who received specialty electrician in Japan, thanks to his outstanding talent could get an engineering degree, but do not become as determined to follow "God's way."

After the Second World War, Moon was convicted in Korea in 1948 on charges of sexual deviations as a "troublemaker" for 100 days, then on a charge of bigamy was sentenced to five years in concentration camps. In autumn 1950 he moved to South Korea in May 1954. founded the Unification Church - the Holy Spirit Association for the unification of world Christianity, and somewhat later (in 1957) published under his name addition to the Scriptures under the name "Divine Principles".

In 1955, Moon came back to the dock. This time on charges of polygamy and sexual perversion: he testified against a dozen women. On one of them seduced by female university students "Rihva" in Seoul, 18-year-old Hawk Hack Jha, Mr. Moon to silence the scandal had to marry. This, according to Moon, "Wedding of the Lamb" was held in 1960. As a wedding present "prophet" gave his bride the title "Mother of the Universe" and the treatise "Divine Principles".

On January 1, 1972 "God" again "visited" Mr. Moon, recommending him to prepare people for the Second Coming. In early 1974, Moon came to the U.S. and began touring the country, explaining that God is counting on America. Several congressmen invited Moon to give a speech at an informal reception at the House of Representatives, U.S. Congress. Got into the press reports that the reception-moon said: "The Prime Minister needs a lot of attractive girls. We will send three girls to each senator. This means that we need them 300. Let women establish good relations with them."

*In the movement of Mr. Moon are,
For example, the following organizations:
Student Association for the Study of the principle (CARP);
International Education Foundation (MFI) - publisher of educational benefits "My World and Me";
International religious Foundation;
Association of Professors for Peace in the world;
Interreligious Federation for World Peace;
International Women's Association;
The International Cultural Foundation;
World Association of the media;
International Conference for the Unity of Science.*

A characteristic feature of Mr. Moon's association - a strict hierarchical structure, with a total subordination of Mr.Moon. The leaders of any activity called "central figures", and to them from the "younger" requires unconditional obedience, "love and service." Thus reliably ensured the unity of judgments.

I believe that this small enough information give understanding that Mr. Moon wrong about the fact that he is the Second Coming of Jesus Christ. At least, this is purely my opinion and I do not impose it to you.

Of course, there is a specific group of people who are convinced that they are the Messiah, but I chose the most, in my view, the visible enough. The rest of them probably somewhere slightly flexing in a small group who looked on them with their open mouth. All this would be funny if it were not so sad...

Benjamin Creme: a messenger of hope

Benjamin Creme (born in 1922) - From a young age he was a student of the works of Blavatsky and Bailey, (and other occultists). First contacted by The Master (full name undisclosed) in 1959. The Master informed him that he would play a major role in the reappearance of Maitreya the Christ. Formed Share International Foundation in 1975. Since then he has been travelling the globe, speaking and lecturing in preparation for The Christ, and he claims to be in direct telepathic contact with both The Master and Maitreya.

Creme's books on the reappearance of the Christ have been translated into seven languages and are published throughout the world by groups responding to his message. He is also co-editor of Share International, a monthly magazine that focuses on the political, economic, social and spiritual changes now occurring globally. The magazine is read in more than 70 countries.

Since his first public talk in 1974, millions of people have heard Creme's message of hope, and many have been inspired to help make it known on a worldwide scale. "My job," Creme says, "has been to make the initial approach to the public, to help create a climate of hope and expectancy. If I can do that, I'll be well pleased."

Benjamin Creme is constantly searching for the World Teacher on Earth and one day he thought that Raj Patel was Him. But it was wrong. Raj Patel is not Maitreya, but the World Teacher is here – and needed.

CHAPTER 17

THE PROGRAM PARTY DRUGG

There was a time when Grigori Grabovoi has given a chance to mankind to choose him as the President by a huge country, although relatively small number of people...

His party DRUGG was in almost all cities in Russia. Recorded on videotape as a rose in unison people in a crowded concert hall of the hotel "Cosmos" in Moscow, when on the stage arrived the World Teacher, quiet and somewhat restrained. The whole room applauded and faces brightened...

It is clear that the Putin government and other former KGB officials and other simply ignorant people have done all that is not allowed to the board of the World Teacher. Thus worked the collective consciousness. So are the dark forces opposing the development of humanity. To understand the level and integrity of the Messiah which is not adjusted to the level of understanding of the majority, but raises it to the required height, I propose to carefully read the program. I'm sure that'll be quite a surprise to you.

The following are the 10 main points from the program of the Party of Grigori Grabovoi:

1. Do everything you can do for the betterment of all people.
 • All energy of the people should be directed toward support for eternal life and well being of the People.
 • If it is necessary to reorganize the State to accomplish these tasks for the eternal life of the People then we shall accomplish this.

2. Eternal Life.
 • Establish a law that will not allow death to occur.
 • New technologies will be created to support this law.
 • All People will arise from the dead.

3. Wealth will be distributed between all People.
 • 10% of the common wealth will be given to all people equally; the rest will be used to support the normal operations of the State.
 • This will allow for a better economy, which will lead to a better life for all People.

4. United under Gods Law.
 • There will be a union of State and Church to realize Gods law not to commit murder. "Thou shall not kill".

5. Everyone shall have the right to work.
 • Technologies will develop new industries to supply jobs for everyone.

6. Proving of social justice.
 • The harder you work the more you will have.
 • You are rewarded for your hard work.
 • Establishment you have of protection for what you have, your earned capital.

7. Guarantee of no more repressions.
 • A look at Russian history.
 • Establishment of laws that will prevent Social or Political repressions.

* Complete rehabilitation of peoples who have been repressed in the past.

8. Education of the masses of the teaching of Grigori Grabovoi.
* Teaching of creative developments all over the World.

9. Safety of the Whole World.
* All weapons of mass destruction shall be removed from the planet and placed into orbit.
* If someone tried to use these weapons they will be destroyed.
10. A union of all of the countries of the World.

CHAPTER 18

ABOUT ILLEGAL ARREST

As long as Mr. Grabovoy had not declared his intention to run for President of the Russian Federation, the media was not promoting material that would deal with criticism and declaring it as a fraud.

There were a large number of publications in various media, they have provided the time on television, and all told only about his talents, and of him as a phenomenon. But as Grigori Grabovoi declared about his political plans, real war opened in the media in which the image of G. Grabovoi was introduced as a proof of fraud.

In addition, during the preliminary investigation, the behavior of operational staff and the investigator was such that they are stated in the form of derogatory, offensive in the form of ridicule expressed in relation to Grabovoi, with his statement that he is the Second Coming of Christ. Stated that he is being persecuted just because he made such a statement.

Persecution Due to Political Reasons of a Famous Russian Scientist, the Chairman of Political Party ДРУГГ of RF Grigori Grabovoi

In September 2004 Grigori Grabovoi declared about his intention to found political party ДРУГГ and be a candidate to the position of President of Russia in 2008. Soon after this declaration leading Russian mass media started massed slandering campaign against him. Mass media including "Izvestiya" and "Komsomolskaya Pravda" newspapers, TV channels ORT, RTR, NTV, and others distribute slander about him and his activities.

Newspaper articles and TV shows produced many times doubtful information about activities of Grigori Grabovoi in insulting and deteriorative manner. They tried to put in doubt authenticity of his diplomas and effectiveness of technologies in order to reduce speed of distribution of technologies of control of reality among people and to remove a possible competitor at elections 2008. Actually this campaign gave no results. The number of people who study and apply technologies of control of Grigori Grabovoi steadily grows.

Later on mass media reduced the essence of distributed slander to false information according to which Grigori Grabovoi and his disciples received money for the promise to resurrect children who perished during the terrorists act in Beslan, Northern Osetiya on 1-3 September 2004.

The press did not write that strange people came to acquaintances and to those with whom Grigori Grabovoi studied at the University in Tashkent, Uzbekistan. These people were offered 35 thousand dollars if they gave incriminating defamatory information about Grigori Grabovoi. Over 4 thousand dollars in Tashkent, you can buy an apartment. These people, offered tens of thousands of dollars for this slander against Grabovoi.

Were spent millions of taxpayer dollars to slanderous company. I got the impression that there was panic in the governing structures. These people are more criminal mafias and they have shown themselves as very active. But they tried to crush and destroy the Lord and Kickback inevitable punishment is only a matter of time. Remember what happened to Israel after the displaying of wrong attitude towards the Messiah.

Hence the conclusion: not indifferent to the phenomenon, as Grigori Grabovoi! This fact alone should motivate the actions of honest and independent researchers.

CHAPTER 19

ABOUT CUSTOMS OF PROSECUTION

About Grigori Grabovoi customs of prosecution were different conversations and different appeared weighty documents. One version was that one of those who were very interested to neutralize the activities of the World Teacher was Osama bin Laden and his people are Wahhabites who were involved at the time of the bombings in Tashkent and at that time, acting on direct orders from Osama bin Laden - terrorist number one in the World. Audio and video with a message of Osama bin Laden appeared June 8, 2006. Payment of a high-ranking officials of the Russian Federation and the media engaged in the prosecution of Grigori Grabovoi and relevant information training was carried out by Osama bin Laden through banks of Australia and through nominees.

Therefore, the prosecution of Grigori Grabovoi made on fabricated data in such a way that even Igor Sechin of the Russian Deputy Presidential Administration on the Regnum news agency reported that the General Prosecutor Vladimir Ustinov resigned because he refused to support the prosecution of Grigori Grabovoi.

Persecution is part of international terrorism because Grigori Grabovoi gives accurate predictions for counterterrorism. For example

On the terrorist attack September 11, 2001 in the United States Grigori Grabovoi gave an accurate prediction and this is almost six months before the events of March 23, 2001, under the official signature on the admission of this forecast, academician of the Russian Academy of Sciences, Savin, and Corresponding Member of RAS Bondur.

On the capture of the Nord-Ost hostage Grigori Grabovoi published forecast six weeks before the event.

On the terrorist attack in Beslan in September 2004 Grigori Grabovoi gave information promulgated in the video seminar conducted in October 2003, before event for 11 months. He repeatedly tried to communicate this information, but no one took advantage of it.

On the terrorist attack in Nalchik on 13-14 October 2005 Grigori Grabovoi with the exact dates of events and the possible effects of nuclear explosions, gave a forecast for the month prior to the attack in the presence of more than a thousand people. This prediction has been used in connection with which managed to avoid a nuclear war in Russia. This is proved by official documents.

In May 2006, five followers of the Master were "honored" to receive this provocative and scary letter. Among the recipients was me too.

-To all the followers of Grigori Grabovoi!
We, the undersigned declare to all of you that the decision of the Shariat Court and the applicable law of blood revenge, Grigori Grabovoi is sentenced to death. The sentence will be carried out in the near future.
A total of 21 signatures.

The fact that it is a fake and a desire to shift the blame on the Muslims in the murder case, it worked in Russia welcome. I later showed that fabricated abomination to Chechen and political refugees, Vladimir Malsagov and he just laughed at this letter. This Shariat Court works differently and does not send such nonsense...
Let's talk about the law enforcement authorities in Russia...
Here's an extract from the document written by a lawyer named E. V.Tokarev. Criminal investigator, M.S. Breev said the following: "You should not have peace of mind. In court, you will not survive. "
And Breev further explained his words in the fact that specific person came with knives to the prosecutor and said that these weapons were prepared to kill Grabovoi during the trial. The fact that no criminal proceedings under Articles 119 and Part 2 of Article 30, Art. 277 of the Criminal Code on these individuals suggests that the prosecutor and the investigator Breev entered into a criminal conspiracy aimed at the physical elimination of Grigori Grabovoi.
According to the lawyer V.V. Rybakov, actions were carried out to ensure the murder of Grabovoi, held in a detention facility. They deliberately made so that the temperature was below zero in the cell for the prisoner.
Illegally embedded in the camera to Grigori Grabovoi particularly dangerous recidivists convicted to use toxins against him, but Grabovoi, using his diagnostic abilities, did not take food with toxins.
This has been carried out, and many other provocations to keep him in custody, because the criminal case against Grabovoi collapsed. In general, the prosecution went for any violation of the law, from simple provocations, right to murder.
The criminal rulers and their lackeys have done everything to break down and even destroy Grigori Grabovoi, but He remained calm and did not softened his position, even after being in the terrible dungeons in Lefortovo. He did not refuse either one of His statements or the Knowledge that the world already has.

To all whom it may be concerned,
From Grigori Petrovich Grabovoi
Born November 14, 1963

STATEMENT

I Grabovoi Grigori Petrovitch, born November 14, 1963 in the village of Bogar, village Kirov, Kirov region, Shymkent region of Kazakhstan, I declare that I, Grabovoi Grigori Petrovitch am the Second Coming of the Lord God Jesus Christ

Without altering any text on radio and television adaptations, or connections with other TV stories, text, images. This statement is made by me, Grigori Petrovich Grabovoi, Second Coming of the Lord God Jesus Christ for all times in any event at any time and should not be changeable by anyone, or ever, or from someone else's name.

October 5, 2006
Signed: Grigori Grabovoi

CHAPTER 20

INTERVIEW with Susanna Dudiyeva

Journalistic investigation of Larissa Bochanova criminal case Number 376 062 "Fraud" Grabovoi / 18.4.2007 2:19
Text: Larissa Bochanova

Susanna Dudiyeva, chairman of the "Mothers of Beslan"
Corr: *Susanna Petrovna, your comments about what is happening?*
Susanna Petrovna: Lawlessness. I say this with full responsibility. Our Russian media and Russian prosecutor's office for some reason, think it's possible to fabricate a case against any person, to slander him, to bear a lie, deceive millions of people and violate the law. They decided that they can do anything. They're doing it blatantly and openly in a cynical manner. But they are wrong.

I believe that we must stop this attitude towards the people by the authorities, corrupt and incompetent law enforcement officials and journalists. We must unite all the normal and sane people to get away from it. And I have no doubt that all the honest people can still do so much more. We need to tell the truth to each other and believe in it.

Corr: *What is your truth?*
Susanna Petrovna: Speaking of the arrest of Grigori Petrovich Grabovoi and his prosecution, the reason for this is based on slanderous articles that state that the mothers of Beslan killed children allegedly paid money for their resurrection to Grabovoi, who allegedly promised their resurrection, that he profited from the sorrow of mothers, etc. It's all a lie.
And if they talk about mothers of children who died, I am one of those whose children were held hostage, whose child was killed, one of those who follow the truth, and leads the people to speak the truth. I am the chairman of the committee, "The Beslan Mothers" and witnessed the whole event. And for the one hundredth or thousandth time, I declare that neither the child's mother, who died in the Beslan tragedy, never paid any money to Grigori Grabovoi, moreover, Grigori Petrovich himself, and none of his students have ever been in Beslan.

In my opinion, all this hog-wash has been launched in order to hide the truth about the real events and those responsible for the tragedy, and to lead people to switch their attention to something else. Here is found guilty - Grabovoi, the whole tragedy and all the grief of the mothers of Beslan, is how we are trying to drum media, is the work of their hands.

This is cynicism in the extreme.

Corr.: *On the investigation of the tragedy that occurred in Beslan, what is the situation?*

Susanna P.: In North Ossetia, until now there are cases in the courts and people are under investigation. Ended the trial of Kulayev, continued hearings on the Right Bank of the district police office in Beslan over the police in Ingushetia, where came the fighters. They came from the border territory of the Republic of Ingushetia. We, the victims, many are doing so that the truth was revealed and made public. Because it does not constitute the truth, not to say that this is correct, it is not correct, so it was, or so it was not. Following this terrorist attack it left a lot of witnesses who were held hostage in the school and those who were around the school. And there are a lot of people interested in an objective investigation. We are very much able to do during these two years, and prove that in fact it all happened. I must say that the delay of the investigation, its bias is based largely on the prosecutor's office itself. That is, who are called upon to uncover the truth that in fact it hides. Nevertheless, prosecutor admits that the federal service interveened when the first fire began. They were shooting in the school where the hostages, with tanks were. Were Established a list of specific names of the individuals who started this fire. Prior to this, the prosecution argued that the tanks were firing at the terrorists, led spot fire on the terrorists who hid in the school.But you imagine how one can aim and fire at the terrorists from the tank, around which there are children, and terrorists are covered by these children? Also, the prosecutor's office was forced to admit that on September 3, they started shooting flamethrowers in the gym, which was the bulk of the hostages. And this has provoked the shooting explosions, because the whole gym was stuffed with explosives. The prosecutor's office, was forced to admit under the pressure from the witnesses, following their testimony. Although it would seem, is obvious, even to us women, far from the military affairs. On the whole, the operation was not properly organized and so was not the negotiation process well conducted in the operational headquarters to rescue hostages from terrorists. In fact, negotiations were not carried out, were limited to some talking and all this time, all those hours and minutes until they're engaged in idle talking, the children suffered, children died. For this should be held accountable as well as members of the operational staff and heads, and this is the president of the republic Dzasokhov, and the head of the Federal Security Service, the chief of the Interior, representatives of federal agencies - Pronichev and Anisimov, etc. There were a lot of generals, army units, all kinds of parts and more ... It was not only the Navy, all the rest of the structures of our armed forces were represented. A rescue never happened. And if, by virtue of authority vested in the heads of such duties, to save people, for that they should be held accountable. These people are empowered to protect the people they swore to the constitution to guarantee the lives of people, so they should be held accountable for everything that happened there. Who gave the order to fire from tanks, from flamethrowers? There are many questions to be answered. Because we see that impunity creates a new crime.

Corr: In *Moscow, began legal proceedings on claims in the media, what is the situation here?*

Susanna Petrovna: The court has already dismissed the second lawsuit to protect the honor and dignity and business reputation of Grigori Petrovich Grabovoi. The first was presented to the newspaper "Komsomolskaya Pravda" on one of the articles written by Vorsobina, second, to the Sokolov-Mitrich the newspaper "Izvestia" article name "Use us in this state, inhumane."

I was present at the last hearing April 2, 2007, and served as a witness. You know, Sokolov-Mitrich was not at that meeting, but it rather was his representative, and I asked him to convey this to Sokolov-Mitrich that after his article that he wrote on our behalf, "to use in this state have inhumanly," all mothers after the death of their children have experienced another shock. And if someone uses us today, it's Mitrich Sokolov, and the like. And after this meeting, I have experienced another shock. The shock of the fact that neither the prosecutor nor the judge did not even try to grasp the essence of what is happening. After all, today the theme of Beslan in the indictment is fully charged, it is proved that Grabovoi never been in Beslan, he did not take any money, for two years the media continue to replicate the same version, although well aware that they're spreading slander. And this is the real information terrorism. Media does not refute this lie. Along with prosecutors and the courts. Cherish what is called esprit de corps. It is because of these articles that Grabovoy sits in Lefortovo. But the court finds that the article did not defame or his name or his reputation, that it is reliable and true. This article from the September 21, 2005, it can be found on the Internet. Yes, go to the Internet but it's not necessary, ask any passerby about Grabovoi, and he recoils from you as from a leper.

As far as the media today, people are zombified into believing that he is a heartless scoundrel. So, in this article, which was discussed in this court, in black and white "representatives of the sect of Grigori Grabovoi appeared in Beslan after the tragedy" or "Mothers of Beslan, chaired by Susanna Dudiyeva went to Moscow to Grigori Grabovoi, which promised the resurrection of the dead children in Beslan caused a real revolution."

Moscow judge did not see anything incriminating in it. He did not see this crime as well as his colleague from Beslan did not see the crimes that the firefighters did not rescue the children, who were already burning for two and a half hours. When the firefighters themselves say that the

Minister of Emergency Situations gave them orders not to extinguish flames and rescue the children, you know? And it is not considered a crime. Yes, we have the authorities themselves criminal, if it goes on like that. Therefore, in the face of all the ordinary people, I very responsibly declare, and I'm sure I heard my son, who died in the Beslan hell, my daughter, who survived, I want to say that sooner or later we will find the truth, and all perpetrators, including judges, prosecutors, law enforcement officials, and journalists, and representatives of government, sooner or later they will be responsible and will appear before the court. In any case, before God's court - exactly.

Corr: *Susanna Petrovna, maybe they think that because of the grief you are experiencing you are ready to believe anything and everything, and deceive yourself in your faith?*

Susanna Petrovna: Who gave them the right to tell me what I should believe? After all, faith is very personal, it is God given. I believe that the persecution against the Teaching of Gregory Grabovoi on Resurrection is directed against all Christians, believers in the resurrection of Jesus Christ. Jesus said, "my disciples will do better than I am." And he himself, as you know, raise the people. Life of Man - The Gift of God and has no price.

Life is protected by the Constitution of the Russian Federation and the laws of our country, so the pursuit of Technologies that give life, which also includes Technologies of Resurrection is a crime against humanity. Therefore, I express categorical protest towards immoral order, and the prosecution of Grigori Petrovich Grabovoi and his students from the media and law enforcement agencies, and this protest will be defended in court. And I have not just a belief in Grigori Petrovich and his Teachings, but there are real results that are strictly proven as the practice is based on scientific evidence, medical evidence. But the media about it does not give any information. They even did not seem to notice it, they did not see the facts. Besides the fact that they violate the law of the Russian on mass media, they also contribute to the fact that these Technologies that protect human life, were not applied. After all, those who are actually engaged in salvation, not in words but in deeds, of those they declare scammers, hang a label such as sectarian on them, are harassed and humiliated.

And there is no need to believe, you just deal with what is happening and this is simply from common sense. When the prosecutors justify murder on ethnic grounds 9-year-old girl, thus supporting extremism and ethnic strife, then what is it? When only the official data of the Russian population is declining a million people a year, it's like? And when we see that the law enforcement agencies, government agencies, public broadcaster spending huge taxpayers' money to combat the teachings of Grigori Grabovoi and his students, how can all this be explained?

When Grigori Petrovich in the presence of thousands of witnesses gave accurate predictions of attacks in advance in Nalchik, occurring in October 2005, thus saving the world from nuclear war. He gave an accurate prediction of pollution of the Amur River in November 2005 and spent the preventive measures, thereby exceeding the allowed rate of toxic substances in drinking water in Khabarovsk.

Why should not I believe this man? Why should I believe the current government that can not even protect my kids against terrorists?

And I urge all of the creative community of the Russian Federation and the whole world to defend Grigori Grabovoi and volunteers who spread his teachings. I believe that the time will come, and we will be happy for the Resurrection of our children. You have a right to believe or not believe, but you have no right to interfere with others. You have the right to stand aside and wait.

Corr: *This belief, which, as you say, from God, as he appeared to you?*
Susanna Petrovna: You know that it is said: "God works in mysterious ways!" This tragedy was the beginning of the search for answers to many of my questions, beginning to explore into a new worldview. Where is the beginning and where is the end? Why is this happening in the world? I am the mother of a deceased child, the rest of my life I will take responsibility for my son. I will never betray the memory of him and I think my mother's duty is to know the mystery of the universe. My fate has put me in front of these issues. I and many others like me, mothers whose children were victims of the Beslan tragedy. We will go to the end. When this all happened, we had a lot of questions. In fact, many children had foreseen this event. They talked about it in their poetry, drawings, they saw it in a dream ... A lot of kids, a few months before, have seen this whole nightmare. We're then all parents, members of this tragedy were gathered, we all discussed it, we realized that the children have felt it somehow ... Zaur Tibloev, student fourth grade, a few months before the tragedy drew everything that happened in September. The figure depicts a school sports hall, all the lights, there are ambulances, still, as it really was. He painted it in May 2004 and died in September. Girl Aza Kumetsova, wrote in mid-August this poem:

I'll go there, there,
Where are all available,
Where everything you can...
I'm tired to wait any longer,
It is simply impossible.

In general, there were lots of poems, a lot of words and stories of children who all sensed and knew what would happen. But then nobody listened to them, did not understand that they were actually talking from the soul's view, what and why they were asking? Why did they not want to live in this world? We asked many of these questions to many people, including the priests who answered, as they could, and explained. And then we decided to go with these issues to Grigori Petrovich. And it was our initiative.

Corr: *How did you hear about him?*
Susanna Petrovna: One of our women, Annette Gadiev, while in Odessa, saw the book of Grigori Grabovoi "Resurrection and Eternal life of the people now is our reality." She was there for the rehabilitation of her one year old daughter, they survived. And the eldest daughter, a schoolgirl, was killed. And Annette called me right out of Odessa, and said: "Susanna, I'm revived; there is a doctrine of the Resurrection!" She said that she bought a book of Grigori Grabovoi that she had seen him on TV back in 1996, but then did not pay much attention to his methods, because then she did not feel concerned. And when she arrived, we all began to read this book. I just read the whole book for the three next nights. That's how we became acquainted with this work. And when we decided to go to him, Annette and I, we did it. Such a meeting would have occurred August 8, 2005. We asked Grigori Petrovich questions, he answered us, and his answers seemed to us far more significant. For myself, for example, I clearly understood that the resurrection is possible that everything comes from God and man, by common action based on love. The love of life, in the first place. The man raises himself, his soul, his love. It is written in all Holy Scriptures and can be guided by the methods which are offered by Grigory Petrovich, but you can just believe ... Actually, it had been enough for me, I somehow easily accepted everything, recieved it in my whole heart and soul, I believe in it, and I look forward to this.

In September, after the anniversary of the tragedy, we were again together with the other women, who had managed to comeby any means of transportation they could: whether by train or plane. It so happened that on September 15, many women of Beslan arrived in Moscow, and we asked Grigori Petrovich for a meeting. This was our second meeting. But on arrival, all newspapers were full of our photos and headlines stating that Grabovoi promised the poor and deluded mothers, in exchange for money, to raise their children, etc. I and the other women have not paid a penny, and no one even discussed the fact of payment.

The same can be said about the TV program "Man and Law". After Pimanov allowed himself to lie repeatedly, that Grabovoi took money from Mothers of Beslan, in my eyes, Pimanov and his program fell very low . They have lost all my confidence.

That's when we realized that someone has a great interest to defame the name of Grigori Petrovich Grabovoi, and that is why they stop at nothing, they even use the names of women who have lost children. We decided that we would fight for justice. Today we filed lawsuits on many media outlets that slandered. This is the "Program Maximum", "News", "Time," "Duty", etc. It turns out that today the media are structures that are just for the money and are not willing to express any opinion.

I do not want to falsely accuse all journalists and publications in these companies, as there are, of course, decent and honest people, but they are becoming less and less. Because the system itself breaks people down. And who dares to criticize us for the fact that we are the first to openly expressed our passionate desire to apply knowledge of Grigori Grabovoi, resurrect our children?

Who and what can oppose us in our mother's desire to fix what happened? We have chosen our path to God, and no one can condemn us and indicate which way we go. We want to get our children; we want to prevent a recurrence of this with your children. We wish everybody a happy life. We wish that those who wrote these defamatory articles about us.

Transcript of the interview: March-April 2007, Moscow

CHAPTER 21

GRIGORI GRABOVOI WAS RELEASED ON MAY 21, 2010

There has been an extraordinary event: Grigori Grabovoi was released on May 21, 2010. I want to bring a small piece taken from an interview with Mikhail Trepashkin, one of the lawyers for Grigori Petrovich, widely known throughout the world of a man who has gone through a very terrible thing, a lawlessness of the Russian penal system, and knows many things from his bitter experience.

- *What are the prospects of the case Grabovoi in Strasbourg?*

-- I have no doubt that we will win this court because the violation of the law in the case of Grabovoi is very explicit and crude. They are at the top. And I'm sure that in order to bring some proof to the case, it will be enough to simply open the document. Here is a sentence, here's how the law treats, and this is what to do. Nothing else is needed. Short and clear.

CHAPTER 22

OLD AGE

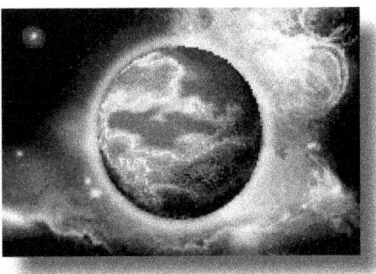

When you type inside the courage to begin to looking at the world objectively, ignoring the imposed views, even if a huge number of people do not doubt the correctness of the prevailing ideas of the century, the picture of the world can be brought to you in person at the root of a non-existing notions of the majority. For this category of concepts, I classified all of which is associated with such a term such as old age. Such maxims such as: old age is inevitable, and so created the world, and the older the wiser, for me, now look, at least hypocritical.

And how often accompanies loneliness of the last days people caught up in this difficult condition! Of course not everything is so bleak, and not for everyone, but let's be honest and look closely at the designated problem: for most of this period of life is not only humiliating, but simply excruciating. I came to this conclusion the hard way: through the long-term observation and analysis. And as a loading dose, on my personal consciousness, has work in rehabilitation centers and nursing homes as a nurse, where, along with youngish, but paralyzed and unable, due to the disease, are kept in very elderly people, sadly antiquated in these medical institutions .It is clear that the weak and helpless people should be treated with warmth and care, trying to make life easier in every way for a person dependent on others, more physically strong and healthy.

The more I watched, the more I felt an inner anger and the realization that "something is wrong here." One day I suddenly realized clearly that all representations and myths created by man over the laws of nature and "the ways of the world", and therefore all people should meekly and humbly accept the existing situation, crumbled in my mind as a house of cards. The king turned out to be naked.

Let me describe an event that was for me a kind of impetus for the revision of traditional ideas.

Several years ago, quietly doing my professional duties in one of Boston rehabilitation centers, my eyes fell on the visitor, a man in his fifties, who was standing in front of one of the patients sitting in a wheelchair, and looking with horror at her. I walked over and asked if everything was okay? What a man, after a long pause, replied that this lady for many years was his boss in a successful pharmaceutical company. And then I looked at the aforesaid lady at the age no more than 75 years through the eyes of the visitor. Before me sat a shapeless carcass fat, flabby cheeks were shaking and her eyes looked dull and pointless on others. With one hand, an elderly woman clutching an old doll, apparently belonging to her in childhood, and from time to time that was making inarticulate sounds. This struck a visitor could not even assume that his dear boss is sitting in diapers for children, and to replace them, assistant of nurses to periodically spend enormous physical, and mental strength to be able to keep the client in clean conditions ... I think, bring him to see this picture, and then depression would be exactly achieved for the former subordinate aforesaid lady.

And only recently I began to understand the meaning of the Dutch painting of Rembrant "The Return of the Prodigal Son," Looking at the exhausted, hungry, in torn clothes son, pressing his chest to a loving and all forgiving father to me, I think, was the clear deep meaning inherent in the story of the immortal artist canvas. The same way we are erring humanity, for many thousands of years away from the house of our Father, where love and peace. We wandered in the labyrinths of his delusions, passions, selfish desires, and the reward for all this - the suffering, pain, old age and death...

The representations embodied in the collective consciousness of the majority of people on the planet are: the aging process is inevitable - it is the law of life and the law of nature, no matter how sad it is to realize. And should be taken the coming of age with philosophical humility.

But however encouraging that recently even the most retrograde newspaper articles began to appear, to put it mildly, unusual. The world is changing faster and faster, and the reality is much of what previously seemed fantastic. According to forecasts of a number of prominent scientists soon people will stop dying, for reasons not related to the aging of the organism. Some of the people living today can even avoid it, and will be able to remain in a state of physical and mental health as they wish.

Modern science knows nothing of a fundamental principle, which would have banned indefinitely prolonging life. The task of cancel aging, has moved to the rank of engineering projects, now the question is rather, not exactly how to do it, but what trends will be the first brought to practical use. Means for defeating aging is a complex of high technology: nano-medicine, genetic engineering, biotechnology, etc.

CHAPTER 23

DEATH IS A VIRUS IN THE COLLECTIVE CONSCIOUSNESS OF HUMANITY

It is considered that in the other world after death, there comes calm and generally we can expect a lot of pleasant experiences, but I think this is another myth and misconception. At one meeting, answering questions, Grigori Grabovoi noted that another world is not as interesting as it is commonly believed. He noted that much more diverse experience and available opportunities one receives while in the physical body.

For those who want to learn more about the so-called afterlife world, I strongly recommend that you read three books by Robert Monroe "The distant journey," "Travel outside the body," `"` Final Journey "you will discover many interesting details extracted by that brave explorer, a man of serious dip in this area. Robert Monroe appeared frequently in the astral world, talked with its inhabitants. He has done for a lot of discoveries about that and wrote in his books honestly and objectively. There is such a funny moment: a young girl who got into the astral world after, I suppose, a sudden death, stood and looked at what surrounded her. Then, depicting disgust expression on her face she said: "This is your much-vaunted, praise, the afterlife world?" After various experiences and thoughts about the finiteness of life and the inevitable moment of dying for everyone, I have at some point realized for myself for sure: Humanity lost, wrongly interpreted the divine laws and chose essentially a dead end and painful path of development.

My logic and soul at once and easily accepted knowledge that has brought mankind the World Teacher, Grigori Grabovoi. Such knowledge can only be from God. Humanity has finally lived up to the moment when the Creator through His Son gives us direct knowledge about the structure of the world and gives the leading Technologies of Consciousness to the Eternal and Harmonious development.

CHAPTER 24

SPEECH OF POLETAEV ANDREW I. DOCTOR OF PHYSICAL AND MATHEMATICAL SCIENCES, INSTITUTE OF MOLECULAR BIOLOGY, MOSCOW

Conference
October 2, 2006

I was on a fairly large number of lectures and seminars, from G.P. Grabovoi. And have been struck from the beginning of the vocabulary he used. The fact that this man, for an hour brings some information, social information, which affects all, but he does not use any negative terms - it is great art, it is an internal gift. Nevertheless, Grabovoi works only in positive terms, is able to transmit the essence of the toughest, most difficult problems that we now face with you.

But mainly, what I would like to share with you is my experience and observations. I am a member of the Academy of Sciences and served as an expert, as an observer, a witness of what was happening before my eyes with my participation. For the most part it's not even about Grigori Grabovoi, but the fact that he transmits his technology and knowledge to others. He opens for those who want to obtain this knowledge. I worked with his students. Most of the experiments, the main findings related to the correction of the health of those people who suffer from ailments such that official medicine has recognized its powerlessness in situations that people face.

You understand that here we are talking about serious pathologies such as cancer, as the absence of any organs, and about of a lighter issues. For example, a person 18 years of age can not be cured by osteopathic obliterating psoriasis. He was addressing to a few conventional medical institutions. And nearly lost any hope. After 2-3 months of work of he and his disciples, personally, psoriasis, against which was powerless conventional medicine - has disappeared. And this woman received a new quality of life. She was under oppression of the long-term illness.

I can give you other examples. A young woman passing medical check-up, received such a result. Blood tests testified that she had acute myeloid leukemia, far gone. Instead of normal blood cells in her blood was found 83% of morbid cells. This qualifies as a final stage of the disease. Very soon the prediction that followed from an analysis of her blood began to be implemented in the clinical picture. Temperature rose and she was in a semiconscious state most of the time. Chemotherapy could not give any benefit already. In fact, the language of medicine - a hemorrhagic stage of acute myeloid leukemia. I beg your pardon, but in the same hospital 20 years before was dying of the described cases of this disease my cousin. And I know from personal experience what it is. A friend asked the patient to the student who practices Technology of Salvation of Grabovoi and asked, if possible, to help in this situation. She asked the student to come to the clinic, to which he said: "This need not. I will assist remotely".I'm not going to take your time describing the details, but after three days the temperature fell, swelling disappeared, appeared a good appetite. She came back to life. She began to recover. Approximately three weeks later, when she began to walk, doctors discharged her from the hospital and expressed joy. I think that the statistics they have improved after that. I must say that, fortunately, this patient did not return to the hospital bed ever. She only occasionally returned to the hospital in order to make analyzes. Six weeks later conducted tests showed that her blood is normal, there are no ballast cells, and six months later she gave evidence and was a happy healthy woman. You know, for me that's a fact which is documented, and a real person living in Moscow, her child is happy that his mom is with him. This fact is to me no less significant than what they say about the return of a person after death and resurrection, because that person actually stood on the brink of death.

Official medicine has recognized its impotence in the face of this situation. The man came back and continued to live and enjoy this life. For me, that fact is a very significant one. I could give many more such facts.

First, all documented by medical institutions, using the instrument diagnostics, biochemical diagnosis, after correction, the correction of non-contact. No drops, no pills, nor spell, nor any other activities not carried out. Work was carried out with the mind of man. These patients are healthy, have a new quality of life. The miracle is this? I must admit, I do not believe in miracles. This is not a miracle. This is the technology. What's remarkable Grigori Petrovich passes on his technology for many people who become his disciples, who then become convinced from their own experience about the effectiveness of this practice.

I have repeatedly said what is happening now with Grigory Petrovich, I mean the fact about the prosecution, which has already been discussed - is a shame for our country. Unfortunately, some countries are going through such shameful episodes as the work of Rosenberg in America, as the Dreyfus affair in France.

Does Russia want to stand and be counted in series of infamous rank? History will remember then, that in Russia it was the prosecution of Grabovoi, fabricated on social order. Let's not pursue Grigori Petrovich, and explore its technology, its system because it has the potential, through which we can become people with a capital letter.

Thank you.

CHAPTER 25

LET'S SEE WHO THE ANTICHRIST IS

By nature I am a researcher, so I understand that every medal has two sides. I am well aware that a certain number of people, even after the recognition of Grigori Grabovoi as a person carrying an extraordinary and unique knowledge to humanity, some will want to conclude that he is a false prophet at best and at worst, the very Antichrist, who is promised in the Bible and the Koran.

The word Anti-Christ, means that a person or persons do not accept of the Christ. And that means they have no objection to the wars, the death penalty, allow yourself to hate your neighbor, does not believe in resurrection, and so on. If these people honestly look at ourselves, they must recognize that are against of Christ, and thus is still an anti-Christ. This people must urgently change their consciousness towards a proper understanding of the laws of our Creator Let the work of instinct for survival, because the laws of karma work very well. I have long doubted whether it is necessary to give a very hard example of how the law of karma in this book. And I decided to share of this very difficult information to illustrate the above.

It was in Russia, the city of Biisk. My mother in law worked at the morgue, she was a nurse. And there was a very rude nurse's assistant who was putting the dead in coffins. And one day was brought a young man whom no one claimed. Then the assistant nurse was told to put him for burial, as the unknown, that she has done in her own style. But the mother of dead young man soon was found, and when she opened the coffin, the corpse was lying with folded neck and legs anyhow. When heartbroken mother asked why this happened, attendant said that the box did not fit and she stuffed the body how it happened. She expressed irritation that many bring all different crooks here and it is not possible with every corpse engage gently! After that, she also scolded grieving mother...

The result: within about a month was killed two her sons, and two these bodies were brought to her shift. So it has provided a great opportunity to bury their children in the same position in the coffin like she did before.

That's how karma works with man, system, state... gets what he made in the past. This is an inevitable law, but to remove or soften the blow can only sincere repentance and action-filled with love. Otherwise, everything will be as with the lady from the morgue.

Why I wrote this? Because I know exactly that we are all equal before the Divine law: and the kings and vagabonds, and the Illuminati and the aliens   Absolutely everyone who has a conscience. So you can not be wrong when the world faces a real threat of global destruction is for the simple reason that the chance may be simply not to be.

I want to write only positive and joyful, but unfortunately in my opinion, we should have diverse and objective information. Personally, for me to study so-called PROJECT BLUE BEAM was painful and sobering. I have also carefully studied a lot of information about the Montauk Project, who are Illuminati, New World Order, Reptilian, interview with Al Bielek. Incredible information that gave to the world Phil Schneider, Stewart Sverdlov, Benjamin Fulford and much more... Impresses scale of what is happening and requires an inner courage and wisdom to make it all right in themselves to assimilate and to continue to insistently move toward a change of consciousness to the eternal and harmonious development.

I highly recommend to find out the phenomenon as the true structure of the earth, which is hollow inside, and teeming with life. Portals in Antarctica and the Antarctic. Reptilians that genetically imbedded in human society.The reality surpasses all of the most daring fantasies and science fiction films which show sometimes Hollywood-often precisely the true information which are trying to hide from us unscrupulous comrades ...

What said Jeane Dixon about the Antichrist

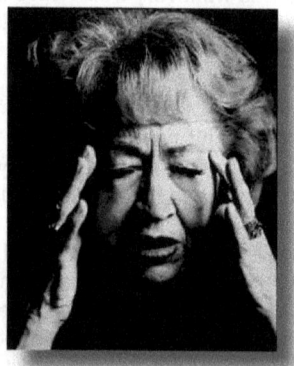

I was unpleasantly surprised that certain writers of articles for some reason decided that a startling vision of Jane Dixon in February 1962 is not talking about the coming of World Teacher, but about the Antichrist. Ladies and gentlemen, please be objective and again read very attentively

the documented text, describing how it all happened and interpretation of the historical vision of Jeane Dickson immediately after the vision. Ruth Montgomery's personal biographer of Jane Dickson very accurately recorded every word in her book "A GIFT OF PROPHECY"
"This person, though born of humble peasant origin, is a descendant of Queen Nefertiti and her Pharaoh husband; of this I am sure. There was nothing kingly about his coming...no kings or shepherds to do homage to this newborn baby...but he is the answer to the prayers of a troubled world. Mankind will begin to feel the great force of this man in the early 1980's and during the subsequent ten years the world as we know it will be reshaped and revamped into one without wars or suffering. His power will grow greatly until 1999, at which time the people of this earth will probably discover the full meaning of the vision."
Attempting to describe her own sensation, Jeane says: "I felt suspended and enfolded, as if I were surrounded by whipped cream. For the first time I understood the full meaning of the biblical phrase, "My cup runneth over." I loved all mankind. I felt that I would never again need food or sleep, because I had experienced perfect peace."

Jeane died in 1997 without having understood who it was who would save and change this world. While still alive, she repeatedly was mocked by the press precisely because of this prophecy, because she focused on it her entire life. Even Nancy Reagan, close friend and the wife of the former President, did not spare Jeane, and expressed her clear distrust.
But many years later, she really had a vision under the joint name the Antichrist. I found especially for those who really want to know the truth and not distort the available information. Let's be honest and do not distort the documentary texts of the great clairvoyant from Washington.
Now, carefully read this text:
"Satan is now coming into the open to seduce the world and we should be prepared for the inevitable events that are to follow. I have seen that the United States is to play a major role in this development... I have seen a 'government within a government' develop in the US within the last few years... I see this 'government within a government' being controlled and financed by a well-oiled political 'machine' of one of our leading political families. With their eye on the White House, I see them discredit any man who occupies it without their approval, no matter how good his political programs may be.
"They will --- through political intimidation, propaganda, and illegal sixth-column activities --- make every effort to show the nation that only their man, the one who heads their 'machine', has the sole right to occupy the White House. Their campaign is going to cause great harm to our nation both here and abroad.

"I 'see' this group succeed in taking over de facto control of the country. They will give rise to an upheaval in our social structure as never before seen. They will bring about increased social unrest and great discontent.

Foreign subversive elements will --- as they did in the 1960s --- infiltrate the unruly factions and cause renewed fighting on the nation's campuses and in racial ghettos

"All of the evil in the masses will be swept toward an unknown frenzy by this 'machine'.

"I 'see' a member of this 'machine' ascend to power in New York City, enforcing new laws and regulations that will affect many households of that great metropolis.

"The social and religious chaos generated by this political machine throughout the United States will prepare the nation for the coming of the prophet of the Antichrist. This political unit of the East will be the tool of the serpent in delivering the masses to him.

"The False Prophet's domain shall be the intellectual seduction of mankind. It means a mixture of political, philosophical, and religious ideology that will throw the populations of the world into a deep crisis of faith in God... One of his first duties and responsibilities in readying the world for the advent of his 'master' is to manipulate the available propaganda machines. With teaching and propaganda the prophet will cause people not merely to accept the Antichrist but rather to desire him with positive enthusiasm to create the conditions of his coming and to participate in organizing the frightful and terrifying despotism of his World Empire.

"[The seemingly miraculous phenomena he will produce] will not be supernatural or preternatural events but rather prodigies of science and human achievements, but interpreted in such a way as to lead men away from God and toward the worship of the Antichrist... The prophet of the Antichrist and the Antichrist himself will be specific and identifiable persons!"

I am absolutely sure that the future offers a lot of options. Sometimes in real life is not happening what was seen by talented clairvoyants. The free will is a priceless gift from our Creator. And thank God we have the opportunity to choose and construct our own reality. That's why many of the prophecies of Edgar Cayce, Jeane Dixon and others have not come to pass. And it is very encouraging...

CHAPTER 26

BALCAN ARMAGEDDON

Newspaper "Your Home Consultant" № 9-10 (29-30), May 1999 article "Balkan Armageddon" - page 2.

SENSATION!

The non-stopping NATO war against Serbia and constant bombing, causes legitimate protests from certain Yugoslavia states. The voice of Bulgaria is especially alarming and repeatedly sends out its official messages to peacekeepers. But the fact is that it is very close to the border, near the Nuclear power plant at Kozloduy, where bombs have already been dropped, and God forbid if the nuclear plant gets damaged. Then it could cause a nuclear Armageddon that will outshine its destructive force of what is already happening, and will be equal to hundreds of Chernobyl disasters. According to scientists, this turn of events can cause the end of the entire earth, both celestial and it's cosmic body. Our Planet, if a nuclear explosion is to happen in this geographical location, would simply crumble.

It is very difficult to take responsibility for such terrible information. Such information was given to us by an academic Raen, a founder of an International Center for the Prevention of Disasters. Russian scientist, Gregory Grabovoj, as early as 1997, with the help of mathematical and scientific predictions, this global catastrophe was averted by Kozloduy Nuclear power plant. The forecast, after detecting defects at the station, was approved by the highest state level specialists in Bulgaria. The Committee, which included experts from the International Atomic Energy Agency, IAEA, as well as Russian and Bulgarian nuclear scientists, confirmed that there is a possibility of an explosion at the second location (?) of Nuclear reactor that could lead to the extinction of life on Earth. And it was not just another apocalyptic horror story. Previously detected defects at that location were the reason why the underground layers under IAEA had higher levels of electrical conductivity. And if the energy in an explosion's crater would go deep, then that place on Earth could have a powerful nuclear runoff. And in simple words, this man made "vacuum" would be able to suck into itself our planet's atmosphere. According to estimations by scientists, by the year 2000, this "vacuum" could have consumed the entire planet and turn it into a dust cloud, and to stop the destructive process would not be possible with any technical trick.

Three years ago this information has been checked by more than one International Committee of scientists for more than three months and fully confirmed the correctness of these conclusions. And now, crazy cruising missiles fly around Yugoslavia along with non-controlled bombs. These games with death, which can only be called Balkan Nuclear Roulette, threaten the entire world, as well as those who take the aim at the towns and villages of the "underbelly of Europe", and to those who command the winged death team to "take off" as well. Armageddon also threatens the innocent people on other continents; orphaned, impoverished, the rich and super rich. It threatens us ALL!

Yes, in front of death we are all equal. And apparently today is the time for "psychiatric diplomacy" to treat the heads of those conductors of war who do not know what they are doing, do not hear any voice of reason, nor voice of scientists, and still continue to play with death and the idea of "the end of the world" in a real, not figurative danger. Would the world population hear about the deadly dangers that have possibly been already prepared for them within those raging warheads?

It is difficult to imagine how humans will try to save themselves if the oxygen begins to disappear from the atmosphere which has been thinned out by the explosion of a nuclear bomb at Kozloduy, as if all going to hell. Will we actually have a merchant of a life-giving gas, similar to one in the "Merchant of Air", a fantasy book by A. Belyaev? Like in revelations of Ion Bogoslov, could bodies of water disappear, and would the earth's landscape really be transformed to look like moon's landscape devoid of the last flower and blade of grass? Or panicking like on the "Titanic", would people be boarding space capsules to flee to Mars?

Today, the struggle for disarmament, for new forms of cooperation and peace of the people, unfortunately has become an empty shell, a silent voice in the wilderness, deafened by bomb explosions and put to sleep by calls from "civilized countries" to "pacify Milosevic".

CHAPTER 27

WHAT'S THE MAIN THING IN THE RELIGION OF GRIGORI GRABOVOI?

The uniqueness of the Teachings is that Grigori Grabovoi does not consider separate different areas of human development, and therefore religion is also not separated from other spheres of life. Here, we see the integrated view of science and religion, and he emphasizes that the word "religion", rather, comes from the word "reality"
In the religion of Grigori Grabovoi the important thing is that every person is a unique world, the worldview of Grabovoi is the science of the mastery of the universe and of the relations in the world. At the core of the Teachings is the principle of macro-salvation, which means the unity of the universe, the relationship of each person with it, each of us, being responsible for the stability of the system.

He came to awaken and expand people's minds to that phase, which is suitable and much needed for the modern man and our current civilization. He came to bring the knowledge of eternity and immortality of the people. Of course, after two thousand years Grabovoy speaks not so, as he said, like Jesus Christ two millennia ago. Since 2000 years, humans have changed and may receive a deeper interpretation of the laws of the universe.

- And what is the role of existing religions and Christian churches?
- Canonical religion was the basis for man's spiritual development. Contradictions between the major world religions do not exist, as they teach the same major moral postulates. The religions have done their job, and now they keep the faithful within certain limits of human morality. We do not believe that it is necessary to eradicate any religious tradition - one must, above all, seek common ground. The religion of Grigori Grabovoi does not advocate for a passive attitude towards life. Does not stand for the false notion that in this life we just prepare ourselves for some kind

of real life after death. It is also false for someone to simply believe that if he will just pray, he will get into the long-promised heaven. Certainly to pray - is good, but you have to learn not to violate the laws of the Creator. This Religion takes us to a new and higher level of understanding of the concept of "do not destroy", "Thou shalt not kill." In general, for many of orthodox believers earthly life is worthless. Grabovoi declares that here and now is our real life, that it has a great value. We need to create Paradise on earth, and it is possible.

- *How Would you most clearly define who is Grigori Grabovoi?*

- Grigori Grabovoi - a Godman with the highest level of knowledge available, the true knowledge and ability from God. Anyone can become as the Son of God, as presently is Grigori Grabovoi. Most often, he gives his ideas freely in all structures of power and all the people. In 2006 Grabovoi wrote an appeal to the leaders of all countries over the fact that there are instruments to prevent terrorist attacks and offered them to pass on a *pro bono* basis, but two days later, was opened against him a criminal case, and two weeks later he was arrested.

- *Why is resurrection the main idea of the religion of Grigori Grabovoi? What is resurrection?*

- The Creator has two technologies for the creation of man: in the form of the fetus and through resurrection. Resurrection is a technology similar to the process of formation and dissolution of the physical reality surrounding us. Resurrection in our understanding - is a reconstruction of the object of information in the form of a physical body. The Creator resurrects himself, and people deserve the honor to participate in this process, by obtaining knowledge.

Currently, Grigori Grabovoi aims to show people who want to accept this Teaching that resurrection could be something normal in our lives. A person can live an eternal life here on earth and where they please. They must learn to move in the subtle plane and vice versa, without dying.

The soul is the highest level of the individual. The soul is a substance created by the Creator according to the laws of eternity. The soul is *firm,* and the soul is the organizational structure of the world.

CHAPTER 28

Sermon on the Religion of the World Teacher delivered in 1999. Moscow. Russia

I must admit that this message led to confusion and misunderstanding even the most advanced followers of the Master.... But we need to have a correct understanding of the situation. The fact is that on Earth, in the flesh of a man named Grigori, speaks the Creator, the Christ.

Grigori-human consciousness is merged with the Christ consciousness. It thereby becomes Christ consciousness. This is a very different level of the individual. This is a cosmic, universal understanding of the laws. Please be wise, abstracted from the personal and feel as a citizen of the divine, universal reality, because we are cells in the body of the Creator and carry within us His potency.

We have been fed for too long with the lies that we are weak and sinful. We were manipulated by the unscrupulous nature and extraterrestrial selfish and soulless beings for millennia. Enough, ladies and gentlemen!

And now, as you read all of this information, I dare hope you take it calmly and objectively, I want to place in this book an astonishing sermon, which was pronounced by Grigori Grabovoi on January 18, 1999, during an individual meeting with one of his students that was recorded. But apparently it was still not time for that information about the lecture to be released and the student just strangely forgot about it and lost it, among the other cassettes and never could see it. But the time has come, and Grigori Grabovoi himself reminded him of it, expressing a request to find this unique record only in 2006.

He was looking for the cassette in one place, but it appeared in another, miraculously,... And the text was made available.

Please understand that the Master never writes in advance what He will say. At the moment of speech the Stream of Knowledge flows directly from the Creator.

Two thousand years ago, in the time of Jesus Christ, the representatives united under the official sign of religion in Israel, as well as many people just considered Him insane, a swindler, and even the Anti Christ, because they could not believe that what Jesus was doing were part of the normal and natural abilities of each person. Jesus claimed that he was the truth (John 14:6) and that everyone on the side of truth listens to him (John 18:37).

" Unless you are God. With God, all things are possible (Matthew 19:26), and again: "I am the resurrection and the life. He who believes in me will live, even though he dies" (John 11:25).

Or even his boldest claims – like "Heaven and earth will pass away, but my words will never pass away (Matthew 24:35)"

: "Come to me, all you who are weary and burdened, and I will give you rest" (Matthew 11:28). And much more.

Therefore, this sermon that you look now at , can cause some confusionin the best case ... But those who have realized that Teacher gives us knowledge of our Creator, will experience rather joy. You are given an opportunity to pass a test for your capacity for discernment. In any case, as someone said of the greats: "YOU CAN NOT BELIEVE, BUT MUST KNOW!"

The basic postulates of the Religion of Grigori Grabovoi. The first postulate

The Creator is eternal, He creates all eternal. Creation of the Creator is also eternal. The actions of the Creator and the created to them (people Note: the author) are eternal.

Therefore, the postulates of this religion, my religion is determined by the path of development in which every action, every element of creation, everything in the world is identified with eternity, and may be eternal. Creator who exists within me He makes it possible to understand how to act in faith and knowledge of His laws and thereby achieve real positive constructive harmonious development. Therefore, a believer in my religion becomes a participant and an accomplice, as well as a major participant in all processes of the world.

And as a certain reality there is a future change of the person in connection with the evolutionary characteristics, due to changes in the world, the main element of my religion is the human soul, the soul, then, created by the Creator and the soul that can create itself.

Acting in my religion, is a believer in my religion.

Everyone in my religion is independent, free and aiming towards creation. Everyone in my religion is free to choose their own path of construction, but it is natural to *party total creative ways of development,* because it *moves sent down by God.*

The regulations of my religion contain the following sections:

First Section. How to profess faith in my religion. There are rules to practice faith in my religion.

The first is the absolute rule of creation at all stages of development of thought and therefore any elements that exist at all outside of the individual.

The second rule is that the creation which makes the individual, applies to all.

The third rule is that a believer in my religion lets it show to others.

Section Two - this is the order to practice my religion.

First - this is an appeal to me, appeal to the Creator, the reference to himself. And seeing the Creator in me, you can see that the same will be revealed to you, which will give you the ability to create.

Section three. Since the beginning the world was created everywhere and in everything and every element of the world has its own value. In this connection you need to think that every step of your development yields and is reflected in all elements in all the universes, all over the world. This means that you are a certain piece. You are a world.

In my religion, you are striving for eternity of the body, and hence making the assertion of the eternity of the spirit, and the assertion of the eternity of all that exists around .

Should be the following aspirations: the eternity of the physical body, the eternity of spirit, and eternity of consciousness of all that exists in the world.

I can say that my religion comes from the fact that I joined the various elements in an aggregate, which turns out to be the real world, that is, I am the Creator of the world.

I can create a world where I want and the world that I want. *But, so I created this world I need each particular creation was filled with the ideas such as the idea of what I have.*

In the modern world, when many systems are not creative, which can destroy, then every believer has the task to display a concrete action aimed at preserving himself and others, as well as the creation of real life.

In my religion, hierarchy distribution of links is as follows: God - He is a True Creator and incarnate in the body, the physical body of Grigori Grabovoi, that's who is Grigori Grabovoi. As a man, he advanced as a man at all levels and, based on the possibility of only human; he shows the unlimited possibilities of man in eternity.

When you look at God, you see the knowledge that He sends you, but when you are present with God, you realize that you are human. Therefore, in my religion, you are that which unites all things in the world at the time of your thinking, development and action. And I am God, because I know it and I spread this knowledge to you because the divine must be the divine everywhere.

So my goal is to show how it is necessary to move, that as a result your every action will then be forwarded to the thinking of God, in God's goals in acting of God. So I open up, open up to you logically, that the faith that you confess to my religion and faith in me, faith in yourself in action, it means that you give yourself development and all at once.

The following structure is called the religion of technology. They are based on construction and religion of technology based on overcoming existing factors in the direction of reality.

That next step in the religion of Grigori Grabovoi is to transform the destruction. Conversion of destruction in my religion, the religion of God, then I think that due to the fact, and so connected and that when I speak of myself as the incarnation of God in me and through the direct process of reincarnation, I am saying that I/you extend this principle to everyone.

Therefore we can say that *God incarnated once, He always has to be incarnated.*

I showed and I show you the way, because I am as a man and having the status of man, because who is more humane than God himself? I show you what I did exactly as a man, and I do as a human being.

What I do you can do, so your goal is to study my work. Also, the study of how I develop, and you will see what you can do to save yourselves and others. When I speak about how you should develop, then I say look at how I develop. When I speak about what should be your first - look at me and see that first for me is the creation of the world. Eternity, which is the beginning of all beginnings.

It is the aspiration, which is necessary at this age, the age of possible destruction, in an age of very hard compositions and very tough situations, aimed at the destruction, is a revelation of thought that is born in eternity is the eternal. Therefore, there is no death, there is no any destructive action, and there is misunderstanding of what is happening in reality. So all of us should realize that the world can be rebuilt and get a completely different world creatively managed, where each person is free and there is no oppression, no barbarity, no killing. And of course, not any forms of destruction, where every object has value in itself, where each entity has individuality and its own development. The proper and only solution is a creation of the world always, everywhere and anywhere. At each stage, you have to build in spite of very different circumstances in life, and who would you be interfered to do it, you should understand that in your every thought and every action of your aspiration shall be maintained for creativity and the truth of creation. Yes, your actions can be tough, can be targeted, including against those who do not promote to or even oppose creation, but your every action should be determined only by the creative thought

The next section is entitled :

The principles of religion, Grigori Grabovoi.

Following in the eternity of anytime, anywhere and everywhere.
I Grigori Grabovoi, the Creator of my own Religion, the Founder of Re-

ligion, which I have called the Religion of Grigory Grabovoi, I urge you to listen, accept and implement, surely appeal to implement the following from my sermon. I call you to be striving for Eternity, which will lead you to a real Eternity. Created space here on Earth, created by Me in all aspects of micro-particles in need of creation, needs further development.

Why did the Creator come into this world for the first time and was embodied in me? For you, to understand what the truth is: a person can do all that the Creator did. The Creator is now at the stage that once people will master Eternity, the next task will appear from the Creator. The Creator will provide the following knowledge, which talks about Eternity in action, the Eternity of love and Eternity in happiness.

When you see that the Creator creates happiness for you, you see that He creates and the love within happiness.

Creator creating you and the world is embodied in the person of His creation, for the first time in the world, when the Creator manifested in me transforms the world. I am the Creator of this, at this moment I am a true man. Therefore, you can create and build world creatively eternal and infinite. I encourage you to do this, because I am, and you have it, when you realize it. You can see that Creator, who is in me and being me, is truly a man when he is among us. You, being with Him, can deify and you can move as it should to move people. The arrival of the Creator here on Earth, shows that you have become people who can express the divine. The coming of the Creator on Earth suggests that you see yourself in my actions and I want to pass you and give salvation since you created the Creator.

So you, being in contact with me giving the truth, which is common to all, as to the Creator, and for you. You created the Creator, so what's the difference between the Creator and you? It lies in the fact that you should strive to what the Creator has already achieved. You have to create as the Creator created. Take a look at how the world is created and exists, and you will realize what the Creator wants from you.

That is important for me, when you yourself are aware of and feel free, you can believe in a Creator who created you, for the maximum degree of freedom that is your true belief in a Creator. Strive for freedom and strive for independence and you will see the action of the Creator, which aims at common prosperity, and universal happiness, as I said, the happiness in love and love is happiness.

The following sermon is called:

"Resurrection of people and never dying."

In the resurrection of the others you see is what the Creator marked an eternity of the world. When you do not die, and others never do you see what is the action of the world and creator outlined this as a reality of the world.

What you see around is your reality, what is within you; this is reality of the Creator. When you look closely at each element of the world you will see infinity, continuous infinite surrounding you. Therefore, any finiteness of that is just designation. Move the conventionality and designation to the side and go into eternity with outstretched arms, chest and head forward, with the open soul. Let Eternity joined in you and you feel that you always are eternal, that you are eternal in Eternity, that the thought that you send is always yours, and it goes nowhere away from you. You have all always and everywhere. Make the world saturated, make more joy, make joy eternal, and make love your very life, make a life in love. You can move as I said. You can move, so I say.

And when you open your hand, then in front of you is what you have built yourselves an eternity. Take it and carried it forward into the light, the light of your own creations and give it to them and you create worlds. Give it these worlds let them evolve forever. Give them a happiness, give them love and send down the love of Almighty, send them the love of the Creator, who now is you.

I, the Creator who created it, am saying that it is. When you do this, I'll do another. Another is that I will show the next way.

Movement in Eternity begins to have its seeds. The movement of Eternity rises from the earth, of houses and of people. And you will move in the direction of religion of Grigori Grabovoi, religion created by me, Grigori Grabovoi, this religion aimed at Salvation.

The path of the religion is the salvation of all and always and creativity in everything and everywhere. Religion of Grigori Grabovoi is that I *practically did, and went himself.* This is what I understood, comprehended and that the Creator became incarnate in me. Religion of Grigori Grabovoi is something that calls you to be saved and you will save. Religion of Grigori Grabovoi is and this is what will confess always, everywhere and in everything. Religion of Grigori Grabovoi is the development in the eternity of all, everyone and everything.

For the first time I proclaim the Eternal development and for the first time I designate the status of the Creator for the creation of my people and the world. I say that you have this status, because when you create, you are no different under the laws of the Creator, and that is the purpose of the Creator, it is the truth of Creator. Creator, incarnate in the person realizes that His creation is the true structure of the world that its creation it is He himself. Creator, incarnate in a man realized that He created Himself. Creator, incarnate in a man realized that He had created correctly.

When you look at yourself and look at your hands, then they will flash a bright blissful light. This brightness is not often visible to physical sight, though sometimes visible, but the brightness is the brightness of your soul that reflects your hands.

When you take them and connect the hands together, you get a symbol of unification, which takes you to the true path. And when you have them opened it is the symbol of union   that speaks of eternity in everything, so the action of this religion is for all.

The next section is called:

"Signs of Religion of Grigori Grabovoi."

The sign of religion of Grigori Grabovoi it is Eternity. That is, any sign, reproduced in any element of time, it may be a sign of religion of Grigori Grabovoi, if the sign is directed at the true creation. So that the sign is a symbol of the soul, as the first sign and is a symbol of infinity, located at an angle.

Convert your thinking, that you transform the world. When you convert thinking you should have time. You must have time to be saved and save the other, no other way you have. You must do this and you do it, so your movement should be only on the movement of my religion.

Grow natural, smooth development, do not make yourselves unnecessary trouble, do not make yourself not necessary conditions that would preclude to the development of eternity. Realize that eternity is like a germ. It must be planted and it begins to rise gently. So take care, look after yourselves, do exercises to your health. Do not compromise your health, always help yourself and others, in all situations save.

The principles of religion and property of Grigori Grabovoi.

The principles of religion of Grigori Grabovoi concluded that when you confess Eternity, you have to advance. Each development involves the creation of a natural environment for health, not the establishment of special situations that test as far as the physical fabric reacts, for example, a person or an object of information in the development process of Eternity

For special effect means that you do not understand the basic principles based on the synchronicity of the whole world. If you develop and test an eternity everywhere, so this will need the whole world, what should be done. Since this development is the movement and checking it stop for inspection. What I mean is understandable if you want to know how much your finger internal, and then do not poke it with a needle, but it is necessary to comprehend the spiritual state of this and find a criterion of eternity in you.

Creator, incarnated in me, He is truly man. After all, who can be more humane than the Creator? And when He speaks through a person this indicates that the Creator does not have any traits between you. He is the same as you, He is a man and you people, He is a man and you are sleepy people, but man understands the man.

Your path is the path that God has shown you. God is showing you. Therefore, each technique and each system of development must be divinely determined. It should evolve so that it is all constructive. According to this principle of building a machine, you must build a society, base policy, the social stratum. The whole development of the whole world. You must send all over the world the principles of the Creator.

Creator, embodied in the person, expresses an action by me as a contact between the Creator and the people. And as the fact that when you pass on this knowledge, you get a correct position, concluding that man can pass it along to all and of course to yourself.

A man who professes the religion of Grigori Grabovoi, my religion, must be sure that he always saves and saves not only himself but all others. Anyone who professes the religion of Grigori Grabovoi can save everyone and themselves.

Prayer in the Religion of Grigori Grabovoi

The first prayer.
Appeal to Grigori Grabovoi.

Grigori Grabovoi, (you can call Grigori), send me joy, love, happiness and dream come forward. Multiply the goodness and love. Change the world so that I can master the next world. So I could see the colors of life, I could use eternity, move towards and understanding eternity.

I must know the laws of the Creator. Grigori, help me and give me happiness, understanding of the Creator, as a truly living and eternal. Give me happiness and understanding of how to find eternity in thy name, How to find eternity in my action and in our action. Give happiness, understanding and unification of the mind of people, give happiness to multiply goodness and eternity, give happiness to the movement of the soul for eternity.

The second prayer.
Appeal for recreation.

Grigori Grabovoi (can be called Grigori), appeal to recreate all that exists and what will be. I appeal to you to get the blessed news of my soul's going on, that I am forever and I always recreate myself, based on the belief in God, of faith in Grigori Grabovoi, faith in the Creator, embodied in Grigori Grabovoi.

I direct myself towards eternity, appointing the blessed path. I define happiness myself and lead others along; I do not create special obstacles in my way. I'm on the right path, where the barriers are not needed. Give me a way of recreation and show where to recreate eternity. Where is the knowledge of Creator to recreate, where to apply and expand my mind. Thank you for ever and ever.

Message to Grigori Grabovoi to find your path of development.

Grigori, I appeal to you to enlighten my way, to give eternity in my hands to spread out before me forever, and my hands are cleansed by it and filled with eternity towards anything I touch. All eternity must be transferred to all, where I am. I want to show other people how I transmit it, I ask that Grigori help me make ... *(At this point, tape recording was interrupted.)*

Human!
You are the world, you are eternity.
You possess immeasurable powers.
Your possibilities are limitless.
You are the embodiment of the creator.

In you, his will resides,
Through his destiny you change the world.
In you, his love resides.
Love all life as he does, he who has created you.
Do not embitter your heart. Think good, do good.
Good will return to you with longevity.
Love will give immortality,
Faith and hope, prudence.

With faith and love
Your invisible powers will come alive.
And you will achieve all that you dream of.
Immortality, it is the face of life.
Just as life is the trace of eternity.
Create to live in eternity.
Live to create eternity.

Grigori Grabovoi

CHAPTER 29

MY RESUME

Someone once said that history repeats itself twice: first as tragedy, second time - as a joke.

In the Old Testament prophecies about sixty major and 270 specifications, which are fulfilled in one person:

Part of the ancient prophecies pointed not to the first coming of Jesus, but in today's Second Coming: "When the Messiah comes, the dead will be resurrected."

No crucifixion has to happen, it's just not needed right now. Ahead of us - comes happiness, and it is no more an illusion. "The kingdom of heaven ..." The Great Writer has probably written quite a different plot. But do not forget about the vector of the free will of the majority - the multiple futures and so there is no reason to relax, fall asleep and take it for granted....

Personally, I know for sure: GRIGORI GRABOVOI IS THE SECOND COMING OF JESUS CHRIST.

CHAPTER 30

CONCENTRATION EXERCISES

FOR EVERY DAY OF THE MONTH FOR DEVELOPMENT OF CONSCIOUSNESS, FOR DEVELOPMENT OF YOUR LIFE EVENTS IN FAVORABLE DIRECTION, FOR GETTING FULL VALUE HEALTH AND FOR ESTABLISHMENT OF HARMONY WITH THE PULLS OF THE UNIVERSE.

GRIGORI GRABOVOI

I would recommend finding some time for the exercises which are cited below. For each day of the month I recommend three exercises corresponding to this day. These exercises contain control of events. For this purpose different concentrations should be applied. During the concentration keep remembering the exact aim you would like to achieve. The aim might be realization of a desirable event, for example, recovery from a disease, development of a mechanism of knowledge of the World, and so on. The main thing here is to conduct always regulation of information for the universal salvation and harmonic development. Such regulation can be a struggle against destruction at informational level because you fulfill the work of rescuers.

Practically, at the level of your perception, a concentration can be carried out in the following way:

In your mind you determine the aim of the concentration which looks like some geometric form, a sphere, for example. This sphere is the aim of the concentration.

Spiritually you dispose yourself to build events which you need the way as the Creator does it.

During concentrations at various objects, at concrete figures, or at cognition of the reality, control location of the sphere. By a volitional effort move the sphere to the area of your perception which gives more light at the moment of concentrations.

I presented one of the variants of Technology of concentrations. In practice you can find a lot of others. The ways of control of events based on understanding of the World processes through concentrations are very effective.

In the first exercise for each day of the month you fulfill a concentration on some element of the external or internal reality.

In the second you concentrate on a sequence of numbers of seven and nine figures.

The third exercise gives technologies of control of events in a verbal form.

For more successful fulfillment of the last two exercises I recommend to know paragraph 7 of Chapter 4.

I would like to draw you attention to the following important moment. You should understand that the effectiveness of concentration carried out by you is determined, to a considerable degree, by your approach to it. Try to be open to this creative process. Listen to your internal voice prompting you how to fulfill these concentration in practice.

You may, as I mentioned before, write a row of numbers on a sheet of paper and concentrate on it. And you may act another way.

When you concentrate on a sequence of nine figures you may imagine that you are in the center of a sphere and the figures are located on its internal surface. Information about the aim of the concentration can be inside of this sphere in a form of a ball. You should dispose yourself to find that number which gives more light.

Having received the first idea that some number from the row which is on the external surface of the big sphere shines brighter than others, you should fix this number. Then mentally join the internal sphere which contains the aim of the concentration and the element of perception in the form of a number.

When you concentrate on a row of seven figures, you may imagine that the figures are located on the surface of a cube, on one of its sides.

Doing this, in accordance with your feelings, you may move these figures changing their location in order to achieve maximum effect.

You may act quite a different way. In your mind you may connect each number with some element of external or internal medium. These elements are not necessarily to be homogeneous. One number, for example, you may connect with some tree, another with some feeling. You decide yourself. In this approach you symbolically equate the numbers with the elements of reality chosen by you. As ever these elements of reality may be not only physical, but mental as well. It means you may imagine them in your consciousness.

These techniques give you additional possibilities of control. You may change the structure of the concentration, your mood to fulfill it; you may vary symbolic equalization of the numbers to the elements of the reality. As a result you will be able to increase the effectiveness of your concentration. You will be able to control better the time of execution of what you resolved. This is very important in practical life.

Your concentration should give an instantaneous result when an instantaneous salvation is required. The factor of time may be not so significant if the aim is to provide harmonic development. The decisive factor in this case is provision of your just harmonic development with consideration of all circumstances. You will get exactly this by means of your concentrations.

So, everything should be individual in these exercises. Everyone should choose independently the system of his development. You should bear in mind the following.

It is not possible to make a choice of a system of your own development just by means of logic. You are sure to set your goals, you aim to achieve them, and, however, your soul has already got the tasks which had been put in before. Therefore, when you carry out concentrations, the tasks which had been put in before can be realized at first. These are the tasks, which were the tasks of the soul, which were not only the tasks of your development but the development of the whole society as well. When you fulfill these tasks you feel that these are exactly the things you should have done first of all, you feel this at a very profound internal level, at the level of development of the soul, at the level of the Creator.

That is why when we speak about concentrations we, first of all, speak about the universal harmony. At the same time you should understand that harmony always implies an element of salvation as a necessary element if the situation requires such interference. However, the main task of harmony is provision of such development of events which eliminates occurrence of any threats at all. It is clear that harmonic development should become eternal.

Concentrations for each day of the month created and approved by me will bring you to this. Fulfilling them you will get that harmony which will make your way joyful and uninterrupted, and you will be able to save yourself and others and live eternally.

Possessing these concentrations you can undertake active controlling actions instead of being in a passive state in any situations. Awareness of the fact, that due to the usage of these concentrations in your affairs you really realize the process of universal salvation and eternal harmonic development, opens the freedom which is given to you by the Creator. This organizes universal creative development together with your true happiness.

These concentrations are given for 31 days. If you carry out these exercises, for example, in February, which includes 28 days, after the 28th day you should go to the first day of March. It means that the day of the month from the list of exercises should always coincide with that day of the month which the calendar shows at the moment. You can fulfill these concentrations at any time of the day. You may determine yourself the number of concentrations per day and their duration. I would recommend carrying out concentrations systematically and before important affairs.

If you find the first exercise of some day rather complicated you may miss it and do other two. You will get the result anyway. Gradually more and more exercises number one will become clearer and easier for you. So do what you understand and what you like.

Now let's turn to the exercises.

1st day of the month:

1. On the first day of the month you should fulfill concentration on the right foot. This concentration connects you with the supporting point in the external world. You lean on the Earth mentally. The Earth in your consciousness is a bearing support.

The control in the system of complete restoration is based on the idea that the supporting point is simultaneously the point of support and the point of creation. Since it is also the point of creation, with the help of this concentration you can develop your consciousness right away.

You realize that based on the same principle which accounts for everything growing and developing on the Earth, for example, plants and even the matter of your own body appear, based on the same principle you may build any external reality. Understanding of this underlies this concentration.

However, carrying out this concentration you may not think about this deep-laid mechanism. You may just concentrate on the right foot and simultaneously imagine the required event in your consciousness. That mechanism of construction of the reality which has just been described will work automatically. And you will receive the desired event in a harmonic way. Because this control simultaneously provides harmonization of events.

This exercise may be fulfilled several times a day.

2. Concentration on a seven-digit number: 1845421;
on a nine-digit number: 845132489.

3. On this day you should concentrate on the World, on all objects of the World and feel, that every object of the World is a part of your personality. Having felt this you will feel that the blowing of the wind from each object of the World prompts you the decision. And when you feel that every object has a part of your consciousness you will see that harmony which is sent down to you by the Creator.

2nd day:

1. On this day you should carry out concentration on the little finger of the right hand. The same way as in the previous case, concentrating on the little finger of the right hand you should simultaneously keep in your consciousness that event realization of which you want to achieve.

This exercise may be fulfilled several times a day. You can choose any interval between the exercises convenient to you. You may start another concentration in 20 seconds, or you may do it in an hour, or a bigger period. You may do one or two concentrations a day, or you may do ten and more.

Rely upon your internal sense, upon your intuition. Learn to hear your internal voice and listen to what it tells you. The above refers to all exercises.

In principle, doing this exercise you are not to be immobile. The little finger of your right hand may touch something. This is not the main thing. Act the way that is more convenient to you.

The thing which is important here is the following. On the whole you have a lot of perceiving elements. Besides the mentioned above little finger there are other nine fingers and many other parts of the body. However there is only one of many perceiving elements you should currently concentrate on, this is the little finger of the right hand. This harmonizes the control. The control becomes harmonic.

Seven-digit number: 1853125;

Nine-digit number: 849995120.

2. On the second day of the month you should see the harmony of the World related to yourself. You should produce this World the same way as the Creator produced this World. Look at the World and you will see that picture which has been. Look at the World and you will see that picture which will be. Look at the World and you will see who you are in this World. This will be the World forever and in perpetuity.

3rd day:

1. On the third day of the month you should carry out concentration on plants. It may be a physical plant, that one which really exists in the external reality. Then during the concentration you may just look at it. Or you can mentally imagine a plant. Then you should concentrate on its image.

A method of reflection is used in this concentration. The main point of it is as follows. While concentrating on the chosen plant you imagine that the event you need is being formed in the light reflected by the plant. It's better to say that you do not just imagine this event, but you really see it, you really build it. The event built with the help of such control appears to be harmonized. This is favored by the fact that the plant to a great extent exists harmonically in this world.

2. Seven-digit number: 5142587;

Nine-digit number: 421954321.

3. Look at the reality and you will see that the worlds are numerous. Look at that World which you need, come up to it and widen it. See it with a look of an eye-witness. Approach it and put your hands on it and you will feel that warmth which spreads from your World. Move it to yourself and look at the Creator. Look, how He tells you and what He advises you. You may compare this knowledge with yours and receive the eternal World.

4th day:

1. On this day you concentrate on crystals or stones. You can take a grain of sand as well. Let you chose, for example, a stone. So, concentrating on the stone you imagine a sphere around it. This is a sphere of information. Mentally you see all required events appearing in this sphere. You just insert the required events into this sphere. By this you implement control while doing this concentration.

2. Seven-digit number: 5194726;
Nine-digit number: 715043769.

3. Possess that perspective of reality which is given to you by the methods. The methods should be harmonic. One method should proceed from another the same way as the second method follows from the first one. Walking along the street you see that every next step appears from the previous one. You may stand up when you were in sitting position, and you see that each movement can be various. It can proceed from the previous action and it itself can turn into the next previous action. Get the World in such a way as if it has always been uninterrupted, as if each movement of this world concerned only you as a single person. When you get that solidity of the World which gives you exact methods of control in this World and of this World, your World will be everywhere and you will come to it and you will take it into your hands and your hands will be that world which holds your World. And you will see that you are getting in touch with the eternal World, with the World of all the Worlds and it will be single for everyone, and this will be the collective World chosen by you and chosen by everyone. Create it to be ideal for everyone and ideal for you. Ideality should not be disconnected. You should see ideality of everyone and yourself in your single World as in the single World of everyone.

5th day:

1. On the fifth day of the month you should concentrate on the elements of the reality which arise as a result of your interaction with other elements of the reality. I will explain what it means.

When you pay attention to some object, by this, generally speaking, you concentrate your consciousness on this object. Due to connection with you this object, this element of the reality possesses a certain degree of your concentration and a certain volume of your knowledge. This object in its turn transfers to other elements of the reality a part of information received from you and something from your state. For example, the same way as the light from the Sun shining on various objects is partially reflected from them, and it lights some other objects.

So, when you looked at some object, it, after this, it means after interaction with you, transferred something to the external medium, something from itself. Thus, your task is as follows: to think and to reveal what each element of the reality transfers to the external medium from itself. You may, of course, stop on one thing. You concentrate on it and simultaneously imagine the event you require. The method is like this. Its peculiarity is as follows: concentration on the revealed by you so-called secondary element brings to realization of the desired event.

So, with the help of logical thinking, or clairvoyance, or any other spiritual methods you find out what exactly the element of the reality chosen by you gives to the external medium after interaction with you. When you concentrate on this consequence, on this secondary element of the reality and simultaneously imagine the desirable event, you achieve its realization.

2.   Seven-digit number: 1084321;
Nine-digit number: 194321054.

3.   When you see the sky you know, that there is the Earth. When you see the Earth you may think about the sky. If you are under the Earth, the sky exists above it. These simple truths should be the source of the eternal World. Join the sky with the Earth and you will see that everything that is under the Earth may be above the Earth. Go towards you spirit and find the risen where they are. Bring the infinity to the truth of the World and you will see that the World is endless. When you see this you will see the true Creator, you will see the real Creator, since He gave you what you have, and you create the same way as He has created. He is very close to you. He is your friend, He loves you. You should stretch your hands to Him and create the same way as He creates. Only Creator-Creator may create creators. You should be harmonic with your creator. You should be open for Him and you should be eternal in all of your manifestations, in all of your creations. Anything you want to correct, you may always correct. Anything you want to create, you may create in that place where you are and when you would wish. There is the Eternity for perfection. For affairs the Eternity is multiplied by the acts of the Creator. You are that one whom the Creator has seen in you, whom He has created in you. However you are also that one who wants the Creator to personify himself with his acts in that infinity in which you see yourself. The Creator who is present in you is that Creator who is moving together with you in each of your actions. Apply to Him and you will have the harmony.

6th day:

1.   On this day you fulfill concentration the essence of which may be worded as follows: change of structure of consciousness in density of concentration due to perception of remote objects.

This way of concentration is convenient to apply when you want the required event to happen in some determined place. Then you need to concentrate your consciousness just in this area.

This method can be successfully used when you vice versa do not want realizations of some situation in a certain place if you understand it as unfavorable. In this case you have to break up the negative information. Break up means detent, de-concentrate consciousness in this place. As a result appearing rarefaction brings to non-realization of an unfavorable situation.

Realization of a desirable event in a chosen place can be achieved with the help of concentration of your consciousness there due to remote elements of your consciousness. We discussed this way of control before. When you use it, you use those elements of the consciousness which are responsible for perception of remote objects. Doing this you can perceive real physical objects, remote, as you see them with your usual eyesight, or you can contemplate remote objects with your mental sight. In this and another case you use the remote elements of your consciousness. And if, doing this, you fix in your consciousness the event which you would like to realize in a determined place, it will take place exactly there.

So, the essence of this method is like that. The more remote parts of your consciousness you use to place the information, the better it is processed and the desirable event is realized more fully. The event will happen in the required place.

Concerning destructive forces the method of defocusing can be used. By defocusing of you consciousness you may make the negative information so rarified, that, as a matter of fact, it will stop being perceived, as if it has never existed.

2. Seven digit number: 1954837;
Nine digit number: 194321099.

3. Having seen the World as if it has been turned over, you should always know, that any upturned; any disconnected or pressed World is always the World of unity, harmony and blessing. You should understand that there is always the God's blessing behind all upturned and ambiguous or non-typical states of the World and you may have this harmony only from the awareness that you have always been eternal and will remain eternal, and no structure, no information will change this will of the God.

7th day:

1. On the seventh day of the months you should concentrate on super far areas of consciousness. In practice we deal with them when we look at remote clouds or far objects, let's say, at trees, or their leaves.

For materialization of some object or realization of some event it is necessary to process a big volume of information. Super-far areas of consciousness provide super-fast processing of information. Thus, the more remote areas of consciousness you use, the faster processing of information you may implement.

The knowledge of these factors is used in this method in the following way. You look at a cloud with your common sight or see it mentally and simultaneously in your consciousness you build the desirable event exactly on this cloud. Or on a leaf, if you are looking at a remote leaf. Due to the usage in this case of super-far areas of consciousness, the desirable result can be quickly achieved.

At that the realization of the event takes a harmonic way. Since the cloud is not able to destroy. As well as the leaf. They are not able to harm anyone. As a result the required event is being realized harmonically.

2.   Seven-digit number: 1485321;
Nine-digit: 991843288.

3.   You see that the World develops in the image and status of your actions in interaction with the God's will. You see that the World is that creation, which has been acknowledged by everyone, and when you want to change the World in accordance with your affairs; bring your affairs to universal abundance and your affairs will strengthen and the universal abundance will come. The Universal abundance is the deed of the World bringing us to the Kingdom of the God and bringing us to receiving of universal life and life individual forever and in perpetuity.

8th day:

1.   On this day you learn to control by concentrating on the consequences of the events.
Imagine, that you are sitting by the lake and watching a racing speed-boat. The water is calm in front of it, and waves appear behind it.
Let's look at the leaf growing on the tree. This leaf can be considered as a consequence of existence of the tree.

Clouds appeared and first drops of rain fell on the ground. Rain drops can be considered as a

consequence of existence of the cloud.
There are numerous similar examples around us. You chose any phenomenon and concentrate

on one of its consequences. Simultaneously you keep in mind the desirable event. And it comes.
This method of control is very effective. It can help to change past events.

2.   Seven digit number: 1543218;
Nine digit number: 984301267.

3.   You see that the endlessness of the line of figure eight joins in itself those Worlds, which you have already met during the previous seven days. And when your World will join all the Worlds, you will see that you are as joyful in your soul as the World is diverse. Perceiving each small part of the World as universal joy you will see that the joy is eternal, as well as the welfare is eternal and in this state of common joy you will rise

up your hands and will see the message of the God's blessing which calls you to eternity. See the Eternity in that place where it is. See the Eternity where there is no it. See the Eternity there where it has always been and you will be the creator of the Eternity in those places where there is no it from the point of view of another person. When you will be seeing the Eternity and will be creating it, you will always be eternal, in everything, in any eternity and in any world. You are a creator in the image and likeness and the Eternity creates you in the image and likeness. Creating the eternal you will create yourself. Creating yourself you create the eternal as well as Eternity may create another Eternity and as well as the Creator created everyone simultaneously.

9th day:

1. On the ninth day of the month you do concentration which can be called as concentration on super-far areas of consciousness in the most approached points of your consciousness. It means that this method of concentration is as follows: the most remote areas of your consciousness you transfer to the most approached ones. This transfer should be realized in such a way that you perception from the most remote areas of consciousness would be the same as from the most approached areas of consciousness. In this case you will be able to get a single impulse for construction of any element of the World. And as soon as you achieve this you will become an expert in control. Since you will have just to be in the state of spiritual mood for everything to be normal, for everything to be good, you will just have to wish so and everything will be like that.

That single impulse which I have mentioned develops a special spiritual state. This state is not exactly related to thinking, because thinking as such may not be present in this state. There may be just a mood, for example, for good, for creation or for establishment of harmony.

So, being in the state of such mood brings already to the favorable development of events.

I would like to emphasize that this method of concentration isolates a special form of perception. The perception is in your consciousness; the perception is a part of your consciousness and you deliberately structure it in such a way that as a result it works as I told.

The given method of concentration affects in-depth issues of control on the basis of your consciousness.

2. Seven-digit number: 1843210;
Nine-digit number: 918921452.

3. Having seen the world as a very deep essence of the universe, you will see that everything that exists in nature, that everyone who exists in nature, for example, a man, an animal, every molecule, or that thing which hasn't been created yet or was created before, everything has one

and the same basis of the God who showed the mechanism of creation of everything. Having seen how to create everything you will be creating everything. Come to this through the beginning of your "self". Come to this through the depth of your "self", and you will see how your "self" develops together with the whole Universe, how your "self" grows up and turns into the World. You are the World. You are the reality. Look at this with the eyes of the whole World; look at this with the eyes of everyone, look at this with your eyes and you will see that your soul is your eyes. Look with your soul and you will see the World such as it is, and you will be able to correct it in such a way as it should be corrected, and you will see the World such as you should use it for achievement of the Eternity. You will always know the way when you look at the World from yourself, out of yourself, and outside of yourself.

10th day:

1. On this day you practice concentration the essence of which can be expressed as follows: concentration simultaneously on all covered by you objects of external reality at a time of only one impulse of perception of all these objects.

You dispose yourself to perceive simultaneously assessable to your perception objects by only one moment of perception. As a result of such momentary perception you should become aware of all these external objects.

It is clear that at the initial stage of practice you may get partial perception of information about all the objects. Take it easy. Really the aim of your work is the most complete perception of all the objects. Gradually you will gain possession of such ability.

However even at the initial stage you will get at least some information about each of them by momentary perception of surrounding objects. For example, just an idea that these objects are somewhere, that they exist.

Generally speaking in order to receive information about an object you have just to find a necessary point of concentration and tune up yourself. Then you will be able to contact any object. You will be able to get access to all spheres of control. And as long as in this method of concentration you learn to perceive simultaneously a big number of objects, this practice will give you ability to control at once big volumes of information.

As a concrete example I can cite the following result of this practice. Suppose, there is a computer in front of you. Having glanced at it appearance, you will already know how to control this computer and what in general you can receive by using it.

The above cited type of concentration will let you get information from any object, because with the help of this practice you will be taught to control any object of information. The access to control may be both logical and unconditional, that is on spiritual basis.

So, for exercises under number one I gave you concentrations for the first ten days of the month. Theoretically you might find further concentrations till the end of the month yourself. This could be done on the basis of cause-effect connections in the sphere of information. You might develop further what you know already considering your work from the point of you of fundamental control. However I will continue setting forth these concentrations, though I will do it briefly.

2. Seven-digit number: 1854312;
Nine-digit number: 894153210.

3. The unity of two figures: one and a new figure zero helped you to see the World initially such as if zero has already been present in figure one. When you look at one and increase it to ten by adding a zero to it, you perform an action. Thus your action and your act according to this principle should be harmonic. You should see that each of your actions may substantially increase, increase quantitatively and qualitatively each of your manifestations. You are a manifestation of the World. Harmonize it together with what you see. Look after yourself and your thoughts. You should be where you are, you should be where you aren't. You should be everywhere since you are a maker and a creator. Your harmony should bring to Eternity. Resurrection is an element of the Eternity. Immortality is also an element of the Eternity. You should find the true Eternity for yourself where immortality and resurrection are just particular cases of this Eternity. You should be a creator of all and everything. You should know and imagine clearly what follows resurrection and immortality, true immortality. True immortality gives rise to the next status of the Eternity, next status of the World and next status of the personality. You should be ready to it and know always that other tasks, the tasks of the Eternity, which are risen in before you and which you pose for yourself give rise to new Worlds which you build in your consciousness, and this World as one and zero form ten, this World is the thing that you will have when you will become eternal since you are already eternal. Your immortality is in yourself. You are already eternal and immortal; you should just become aware of this. Get over to this level by the way of a rational action similar to joining of one and zero and you will get this immortality in each of your actions, in each of your manifestations, in each of your steps.

11th day:

1. On the eleventh day of the month you concentrate on phenomena which reveal interaction of animals with man. For example, you have a dog, or a cat, or some bird, let's say a parrot, living in your house. Think, what is the deeper sense of this interaction, these contacts, and this communication? It's from your point of view. And what about their point of view?

When you become aware of the processes of perception and thinking of other participants of interaction you will be able to enter the structure of control of the reality.

    2.   Seven digit number: 1852348;
Nine-digit number: 561432001.

    3.   Just as you increased one ten times by adding one round figure zero, you will receive the next number by adding figure one to one. Number 11 is personification of the World which is inside of you and which is visible to everyone. You are that essence which is always visible to everyone and everyone can get your harmonic experience, that one which you received in your development. Share your experience and you will get the eternal life.

12th day:

    1.   On this day you concentrate on phenomena which can raise a question on creation of the whole. For example, a goose or a swan lost a feather. In this case you have to concentrate on thought what should be done in order to return it to the original place. How this could be achieved? It means you try to understand how the single whole can be created or reconstituted.

Or, let's consider another example: a leaf fell from the tree. What should be done to get it returned to its original place in order to have the tree with it in its initial appearance?

This is concentration on collection of separate elements of reality to single whole, which is their norm. Practice in such concentration provides control.

In this concentration as well as in many others you may consider yourself as an object. You can restore any of your organs. A woman once applied to me. During a surgery she had a womb cut out. You understand how important this issue is. I applied those methods and principles which you are now aware of, and now this woman has a full healthy womb.

    2.   Seven digit number: 1854321;
Nine digit number: 485321489.

    3.   Join with the World in its covering, with that as you perceive it in your acts, and you will see that your acts are that essence of the World which harmonizes with you everywhere and always. And you will see that, having sent to you the God's blessing, the God wanted the unity from you. You should have the unity where the God has development. The unity with the God is in the development. In the development Godlike, true and creative, the unity comes in every moment of your movement. You move and develop towards the Eternity and this will be your unity forever with the Creator in your eternal development. Eternity of life this is the true

unity with the Creator.

13th day:

1. On the thirteenth day of the month you should concentrate on discrete, separate elements of some object of the reality.

Suppose you perceive some object. It may be, for example, a truck, or a palm, or a stone. It doesn't matter what object it is. The main thing in this case is that in the chosen object you deliberately isolate some of its fragments, some parts. A truck, for example, can be imagined as consisting of many separate parts.

I would like to remind you, this can be done with any forms, which are not the forms of a man. It is not possible to do this with a person. A person should be always perceived as a whole. It's a law.

If the object chosen by you is not a person but something else, or a truck, you may imagine it consisting of separate parts. So, your task here is to find connections existing between separate parts. And when you find these connections and simultaneously keep in mind the event you need, for example, healing someone or acquiring the ability of clairvoyance you achieve realization of this event. In such a way you can perfect your abilities in control.

2. Seven digit number: 1538448;
Nine digit number: 154321915.

3. You will see those faces which created the World before you. You will see those mechanisms which created the World before you. You will see the World which had been before you. And you will feel that you have always been, transfer this feeling to these faces and with this feeling create these mechanisms. And you will see that everything around you artificially reproduced or naturally created, that all this is the Creator. He personified you in everything that you see. Your personification is that World which is being created. In such a way you can find any technology of spiritual, intellectual, man-caused and whatever you like, but for sure creative development. Look at the development as at equal in rights universal development of any element of reality and any object of information and you will see that essence which is your soul, your personality and your Creator. Individuality of the Creator and creation by Him of everyone underlay the World harmony, which is inherent in everything, has always been and understandable everywhere. The Creator who has created you and only you individually has created everyone at once. Do the same way, create the World individually and at once simultaneously for everyone and for all times and spaces.

14th day:

1. On this day of the month you concentrate on the movement of the objects surrounding you. You watch them and ask yourself a question: Why is the cloud moving? Why is it raining? Why can the birds fly? Why altogether is all that happening? You try to find for yourself informational essence of each event.

When you concentrate and simultaneously keep in mind the required event, you achieve its realization. And simultaneously you perfect yourself in the mastery of control.

2. Seven digit number: 5831421;
Nine digit number: 999888776.

3. On this day you should see your hands as hands reflecting the light of life. On this day you should see your fingers as fingers reflecting the light of the hands. On this day see your body shining with bright light of the Creator, shining with the bright light of love, good and health for everyone, shining with bright light of my Teaching about eternal life. On this day you may feel this Teaching about eternal life, my Teaching, and apply to me in your mind. You may also apply to me on any other day and in any other state, and you can always ask anything that you want for getting eternal life and universal creation. Apply to me and you will get help. You may also apply to yourself and independently learn what you have received from me. You may see this knowledge and use them and show to others. On this day you may be in harmony with me the same way as you may be in harmony with me on any of the previous days and on all subsequent days. On those days when the time will not be measured with time and space you will also be able to apply to me and you can always come out with a request for help, with a request about conversation, with a request about an event or just in order to apply. You are free as you have been always free. Make it a rule, distribute this rule to others and you will get eternal life wherever I am. And you will get eternal life wherever you are. You will get eternal life wherever everything is. And you will get eternity wherever everything is and has always been. And this principle will be trustworthy and true for everyone, and it is trustworthy and true for everyone, and you are that one who you are in the Eternity, because you are the Eternity.

15th day:

1. On the second day of the months you practiced concentration on the little finger of the right hand. On the fifteenth day you can use for this purpose some other parts of your body, for example, other fingers, or nails, or something else at your discretion. Further on the concentration is carried out the same way as I explained it for the second day.

2. Seven-digit number: 7788001;
Nine-digit number: 532145891.

3. On this fifteenth day of the month you can feel this God's blessing which is sent down by the Universal mind, which is itself grateful to the God for its creation. For creation of every of its elements and for creation of such of its status that it can reproduce the Universe, since the God is present everywhere. And due to this principle feel the gratitude of a plant and an animal towards you, feel the gratitude of another person and feel their love. And you will see that you love them. The love includes creation, blessing and universal penetration. And common love, achievable by everyone and achieving everyone, this is the Creator, who personified the World in your manifestation. You are a manifestation of love of the Creator, since He is the love in relation to you. You initially received the Creator's gift and you are him, you are a creator, because you are created by the Creator, by the eternal and all-embracing God; go that way, where He is, since he is everywhere. Go that way where He calls, since He calls everywhere. He is where you are, He is everywhere where you are. You are in the movement of the Creator; you are a personification of His Eternity. Go along with the concerns of the Creator, He created the eternal World in universal mutual development, and you will see that the World personifies eternal you. You are a creator who creates the eternal and the Creator created you eternal when creating the eternal World.

16th day:

1. On this day you concentrate on the elements of the external reality which contact your body.

Since childhood we have remembered a wonderful phrase, "The Sun, air and water are our best friends". In this concentration you are trying to become aware of interaction with these of our friends.

You concentrate on the warmth which is given by the beams of the Sun falling on you. You feel their touch; you feel the warmth given by them.

You feel a light wind blowing on you. You feel its breaths. This may also be strong blasts of wind. This may be quite immovable air. And if at the same time it is very hot and the humidity is high, you simultaneously feel warmth, air and moisture on your cheeks.

You may enjoy refreshing action of the water when you wash your face, take a shower or swim.

These concentrations can be also done in the cold winter time. During a warm season, especially in summer at a beach, all your body can enjoy the contact with the sun, air and water. A contact with the ground can be added here.

These concentrations are very important. Doing them you enter deliberate interaction with the elements.

It is clear that you can do this practice every day. If, during the concentration, you simultaneously keep in mind the required event, you achieve its realization.

2. Seven-digit number: 1843212;
Nine-digit number: 123567091.

3. Feel the harmony where it is, and it is everywhere and always. This is the harmony of the Creator. Feel the harmony where it is and will be. This is the harmony of your development. Feel the harmony where it is, was and will be, and where it wasn't, isn't but where it will always be. This is the harmony of change. This is the harmony of transformation. This is transformation into eternal life. Come to yourself everywhere, and feel this harmony everywhere, and you will see how the waves of joy and love emanate from your harmony. And you will see that you make the World harmonic forever in its eternal status of stability. You are the fighter, but in eternal God's blessing for eternal life and eternal faith.

17th day:

1. On the seventeenth day of the month you concentrate on the elements of the external reality which, from you point of view, always surround you. This is the space surrounding you, the Sun, the Moon, known to you constellations and altogether everything that, based on your understanding, always exists. You concentrate on any of these elements and simultaneously, as ever, keep in mind the required event for its realization.

2. Seven-digit number: 1045421;
Nine-digit number: 891000111.

3. Look with the all-seeing eye after resurrection of everyone and everything. And you will see that restoration of the World is that reality in which you live. And you will feel that you are in the eternal World. Move along this path forward and you will see the way which calls you. Go along this way and you will see the Creator who is eternal and you will enjoy your eternity; and this enjoyment is the eternity of life; and the Creator is exactly that Creator who created you; and His love is infinite; and His simplicity is trusting and he is as simple and transparent as you have imagined, as you thought about Him before; and He is as kind and constructive as you knew it before. He is your Creator and He gives you the way. Go along His way, since His way is your way.

18th day:

1. On this day of the month you concentrate on immovable objects. This may be a building, a table, a tree. Choose anything you like. Further on you have to find the individual essence of the chosen object, its meaning. The essence for you means that you should understand what this object for you is. Such is this concentration.

In future when describing the exercises I will not be mentioning that that during the concentration you should keep in your consciousness the required event in order to control it. In future it will be always meant.

2. Seven-digit number: 1854212;
Nine-digit number: 185321945.

3. You go that way, where people are. You go that way where the events are. You work where the resistance is. And when you see this the resistance becomes transparent, its strengths weaken and you see the World of the Eternity even if the resistance is still present. Go and be everywhere, where you want. You can be everywhere. You can embrace the whole world of welfare; that is why, you should fight with the resistance for the welfare of the eternal life; and the resistance will break down and you will see the light of the eternal life and you will perceive it. And this will be realized forever and all times.

19th day:
1. On the nineteenth day of the month you should concentrate on phenomena of the external reality, in which something, which preliminary had existed as a single whole, turns then into aggregate of separate elements. An example of such phenomenon is a cloud which turns into rain drops. Or another one: the crown of a tree turns into separate falling leaves.

Throughout the concentration on such phenomena you are trying to find the laws due to which such development of the event could be prevented. To find such laws is the sense of this concentration.

2. Seven-digit number: 1254312;
Nine-digit number: 158431985.

3. The struggle of the spirit for its true place in the World, as well as the struggle of your soul for personification of the Creator, make your intellect and your mind controlled. Your consciousness becomes universal and your part of the consciousness becomes the common consciousness. You become who you are. Your eternity is revealed in your thoughts, your contemplation becomes eternity, your thoughts make the World eternal and you will be where you are, and you will be where you aren't, and you

will always be, though the World consists of time intervals, and where you will be the time interval will become the World and the space will join the eternity, and the time will retreat and you will be in movement and you will be in eternal time, and you will feel the eternal time, and this eternal time will come to you. Every moment of your time is an eternal one. Feel the eternity in every moment and you will see that you have already got it.

20th day:

1. On this day you should concentrate on remote areas of consciousness. Your task is to help other people.

Imagine that you want to explain something to another person. To explain what he doesn't know or doesn't understand. As a matter of fact we know already that in reality every person possesses all knowledge, his soul initially has everything. That is why your task is to help him to realize information which he has already got. By the way, the genuine understating is exactly connected with awareness of the knowledge available in the soul.

The easiest way to awake a person to awareness of required information, kept in his soul, is through the remote areas of his consciousness. The easiest way to reach them is through remote areas of your consciousness.

Doing these exercises you already actively participate in the salvation program. In this respect I would like to specify what should be the fundamental thing for your concentration. Your concentration should give such control which could provide positive effect for everyone at once; it should provide favorable development of events for everyone at once. This doesn't depend on location of other people. Physically people may stay at a big distance from you; anyway they will receive help from you.

To be more precise this exercise may be called as concentration on the common success. I mean that due to your work, development of specific situations will take favorable direction for everyone.

Would you wish it, especially at the initial stages in the beginning of your practice, one more exercises can be added on this day.

You concentrate on such remote objects such as the Sun, planets or stars and constellations. You may not see them with your usual sight. Your task in this concentration is as follows: you try to understand what these objects are from the point of view of information.

2. Seven-digit number: 1538416;
Nine-digit number: 891543219.

3. Look at the world from the highest position of your consciousness, from the deepest position of your soul and the most spiritual passion to universal welfare, look at the World in such a way as if it is just being created and create it as it is now. However, creating it as it is, change simultaneously the state of the World with its vices for the better, towards

creation and eternal life. And you will see that the vices are not the vices at all, but a wrong understanding of the World. Understand the World correctly as it is given to you by the Creator, and you will see that the Creator is everywhere and the correctness is everywhere, you should just make one step towards, you should just not negate and come to this correctness forever and for good and you will see that the World has transformed. And you will see that the universe became yours, and you will see that the Creator is pleased with you, and you will see that you are a creator and able to create everywhere, always and forever, and you are a helper of the Creator, and you are a helper of anyone else and you, as the Creator himself, are creating a creator and here you come to the point of unity of everyone. And this point of unity of everyone is just your soul. Look at it and you will see the light of life. This light of life is created by your soul. The luminescence of your soul is the thing which calls you upwards, afar, and in breadth, the luminescence of your soul is the World. You see the World because your soul sees it. You see the soul because you have eyes of the soul. Look at yourself from all sides, and you will see common joining with the entire World, with the entire World which exists everywhere and always. Your thought is the thought of the World. Your knowledge is the knowledge of the World. Distribute the knowledge of life and distribute the light of your soul, and you will see the eternal life in such a state, in which you are in it. You will see that the eternal life has been with you for a long time; it always is, was and will be. The eternal life is you.

21st day:

1. On the twenty first day of the month you should concentrate on the series of numbers, going in reverse sequence. A specific example: 16, 15, 14, 13, 12, 11, 10. Numbers appearing in these sequences should be within the row from 1 to 31 (maximum number of days in a month.) So, there are 31 numbers at your disposal. When you compile sequences from these numbers rely upon your internal feeling.

2. Seven-digit number: 8153517;
Nine-digit number: 589148542.

3. Watch how a mountainous stream runs down the mountains. Watch how snow melts. Look mentally at these pictures, if you have seen them with your eyes. You will see that your thoughts do not differ from your eyes. And you will see that your consciousness doesn't differ from your body. And you will se how your soul builds your body. Don't forget this knowledge transferring it from one second to another and turning a moment into eternity you will be building yourself eternally, as you without any efforts lived before, and thus this eternal construction is the eternal life. Build around yourself on the basis of the same principle other objects,

build worlds. Create joy and sow wheat, create bread, give tools and give machines and make machines harmless, not destroying and you will see that you live in this World, and you will see that this is sent down to you and that the God and your consciousness are revealed in this machine. Stop a machine if it threatens. Build the body if it is ill; realize resurrection if someone has passed away, prevent anyone else from passing away. You are a creator; you are a maker, take, act and go forward in harmony with the entire World, in harmony with everything created, in harmony with everything that will be ever created in the entire eternity and in manifestation of the World, and in harmony with yourself.

22nd day:

1. On this day of the month you should concentrate on such elements of reality which are characterized by the endless reproduction. A specific example: a notion of eternity. Or a notion of endless space. I would like to remind you once again that thinking, for example, about eternity you at the same time should construct the required event.

2. Seven-digit number: 8153485;
Nine-digit number: 198516789.

3. Your soul is a created structure; your soul is a recreated structure. Watch how your soul is being created, watch, how it is being recreated. Your Soul is in the act of recreation, open your world and look, where the Creator has recreated himself, look at the mechanism of recreation and you will see love. Love is the thing which brings light to the world. Love is the thing on which the world is being built. Love is the thing that always exists and had initially been. Look at that one who created love and you will see yourself. Love belonging to you it is you belonging to love. Build with love, build with welfare, build with a great joy of universal life and universal happiness and you will be able to see that joy which is seen by everyone who is around you. See the joy of those who are around you and your heart will be filled with happiness. Be in happiness; be in harmony and this happiness will bring you eternity. Look with your eternal eyes, look with your eternal body, and look with your eternal look at your relatives and grant them Eternity. Look with your Eternity at all people and grant them Eternity. Look with your eternity at the entire World, at all your environment and grant them Eternity. And the World will blossom and a flower which blossoms eternally will appear. This flower will be your World which is the World of everyone. And you will live and your happiness will be endless.

23rd day:

1. On the twenty third day you should concentrate on development

of all elements of reality towards realization of the tasks of the God.

2. Seven-digit number: 8154574;
Nine-digit number: 581974321.

3. Look at the World, what should be done in it, look at you everyday affairs, see your feelings and look at them. Look, how your feelings are connected with the events, why are you looking forward, why do you feel, why do your affairs go in such a way but not another. Why can the words "another way" not be present in the World, since the World is single and it is various in its singularity? Why does the word "single" mean variety? Feel the entire nature of phenomena in your specific case. Look at this case from all sides. Look at your organism and restore it with one mental moment. Look at your consciousness and make it able to solve all your issues. Look at your soul and see that everything has been available there for long time.

24th day:

1. On this day of the month during concentration you should receive any object from a form of a man. For example, a video-cassette, a fountain-pen, a plant. You should see from what element of the man's body appears, let's say, a video-cassette. It means how to realize the image of a man in order to receive a video-cassette.

2. Seven-digit number: 5184325;
Nine-digit number: 189543210.

3. You have seen that reality, which you have seen. You have come to that reality, which you are. Look at all days from the first to twenty fourth and you will see that your love is endless. Look at the world, how you look with love, look at the feeling, how you build it, look at the feeling as at the eternal creation and you will come to love as if to Eternity. You come to it forever and you stay with it forever. The Creator, your God created you as loving persons. You are the God's creations and you love. Love is life, and life is love. Display love where you appear, display love in those places where you determine yourself, and predetermine yourself. Love may be not expressed by words and love may be not expressed by feelings, however your actions are love where you create.

25th day:

1. On the twenty fifth day of the month you may concentrate on any objects at your choice, however it is important to have several various concentrations in order to have a kind of an aggregate concentration. Having analyzed this aggregate you join various objects of concentrations

into groups based on some sign. For example, a tape-recorder and a cassette can be placed into one group because they add one another when they fulfill the task they are meant for. A tape-recorder and a receiver can be joined into one group which you consider as goods produced on the basis of electronic equipment. One group can include objects of the same type, for example, two different books. However, if to consider these books from the point of view of their content, these books may appear in different groups if combination of groups will be based on the content. You see, you have complete freedom of creation in this case.

You may, for example, sitting at home, look around and use objects surrounding you for this concentration.

2. Seven-digit number: 1890000;
Nine-digit number: 012459999.

3. Come to the thought about yourself. Catch the thoughts about yourself as reflection of yourself. See yourself as you see all people. See yourself as you see everyone. See yourself as you see a branch of a tree, a leaf of a plant, morning dew or snow on a window-sill. You will see those things which are eternal before you. You will see that you are eternal.

26th day:

1. On this day of the month you learn to see simultaneously the whole and a part of it, the common and particular.

Suppose, there is a herd of cows in front of you. You see the whole herd and simultaneously can concentrate on any cow. And understand how it lives, what it thinks about, how it will develop. Or you may look at an ant hill and simultaneously at some ant.

With the help of this concentration you should understand how practically with one look you can see at once the whole and its part, the common and particular. This concentration will help you to acquire this ability. You will be able to see instantly both common and particular.

2. Seven-digit number: 1584321;
Nine-digit number: 485617891.

3. Take into consideration that you develop eternally. See that your development is eternal. Busy yourself with all that is eternal. Since each movement is eternal, and each thing is a personification of the Eternity, and each personality is the Eternity, and each soul is a multitude of Eternities. Go towards diverse Eternities from the single Eternity and you will see that there is one Eternity for everyone. Come to this through understanding of your soul and you will see that you are the creator of anything you need. Apply this to creation of each thing and you will see that each thing has been created by you. Apply this to creation of your

organism and you will see and you will understand that your organism can always be self-healed. Apply this to the health of others and having cured another one you will gain experience for yourself. Curing of others is always an experience for you. Restoration of everything is always an experience for you. Be good to more and more people, give more joy and happiness and you will get the Eternity into your hands in the form of a concrete technological tool of your consciousness. Spread the consciousness to the rigid conditions of the Eternity. There, where the Eternity widens, outrun it, outrun the Eternity in the infinity and you will see yourself as a personification of the Creator. You create in that place where the Eternity is just widening, you are the creator of the Eternity, you control the Eternity and the Eternity always obeys you.

27th day:

1. On the twenty seventh day of the month you should do the same concentration as on the ninth day of the month, but add to it an infinite development of each element of the concentration.

2. Seven-digit number: 1854342;
Nine-digit number: 185431201.

3. Come to help to those who need help. Come to help to those who do not need help. Come to help yourself, if you need help. Come to help yourself if you do not need help. Look at the word "help" in its wider manifestation and look at the kindness as personification of help. You are kind and you help. You are a creator and you have help. Every act of your consciousness brings help to you. Everything created by you is a help to you. You have an infinite number of helpers as well as you help to an infinite number of others. You are in universal connections with everyone, you always help everyone and everyone helps you. Being in universal connections and mutual help bring the society to the welfare, give happiness to everyone and you will see yourself in universal world harmony with everyone where the God-Creator is everything that has been created around you; it's everything that has been created by you and personification of the God in everything created around you. Personification of the God as your creator will reveal in your soul as a genuine understanding of the World in self-development after getting the infinity of life.

The infinity of life is the infinity of the Creator. To be infinitely living you should be being infinitely created, you should be infinitely created. You may do so that every your thought, every your movement, every your action created the Eternity.

28th day:

1. On this day of the month you should fulfill the same concentration as on the eighth day of the month but with one important difference. The thing is as follows.

You must have noticed that on the previous day, 27th, when determining the type of concentration the numbers 2 and 7 were added: 2+7=9. In this case the situation is different.

The number 28 consists of two figures: 2 and 8. In this case the number 28 should be perceived as follows: two multiplied by eight. Not to add 2 and 8, but just multiply. It means that eight is doubled. That is why the program of the eighth day is repeated on this day.

However this repetition should not be strict, it shouldn't be an exact copy of the previous work. You have to change something. And first of all change something in yourself. For example, change something in your vision of this concentration. Fulfilling it according to the old scheme you should nevertheless see something new in it, to look at it from another side.

Your understanding as well as your perception of these concentrations should be always widening and deepening. This is a creative process. It facilitates your development.

2. Seven-digit number: 1854512;
Nine-digit number: 195814210.

3. Look at yourself as you look at the whole World right away. Look at the Creator the same way as the Creator looks at you, and in this get understanding what the Creator wants from you. Look at His look and you will see His look. You will see that the look of the Creator is also fixed at the far phenomena of the World; and your task is to control these phenomena of the World. You should make harmonic any phenomena of the World. This is your true task. You should give birth to the Worlds and crate the Worlds which will always be harmonic. This has been your true task since your creation. Since He, the Creator, has already created, since He, the Creator, has already done, and your task is to go along this way since you have been created in the image and likeness the same way as the Creator has been created. The Creator created himself and He created you as well. Create yourself and create others. Create all others and give universal welfare to everyone and you will have the World which has been created for you, and for everyone, and for the Creator. Create for the Creator since He created you. Create for the Creator since He created everything. That is why whenever you create anything you create for the Creator.

29th day:

1. On the twenty-ninth day you fulfill a resumptive concentration.

On this day you should look at all concentrations of this month from the first day to twenty-eighth. However you should perceive them in an impulse. It's important. The way covered within the month you take in with one single moment of perception.

At this you should do a certain analysis of your work. On this day you so say create a platform for the work in the following months.

You may imagine everything you have done in the form of a sphere which you should place on an endless straight line the initial part of which includes the following month. Thus you create a platform not just for the next month but for your further infinite development as well.

2. Seven-digit number: 1852142;
Nine-digit number: 512942180.

3. Look at the World with your eyes. Look at the World with all of your feelings. Look at the World with all of your cells. Look at the World with your whole organism and with everything with what you can see and with everything you are. Look at the World and yourself and inside of yourself. Look at the World understanding that the World is around you and it envelopes you. Look at the reality which gives life. Look at such reality which gives the Eternity. And you will see that whatever you look at there is only this reality that gives life and gives the Eternity. And the creator of this reality is the God. The God who has created this reality has created the eternal life and he sees you the same way you see yourself, and he sees you the same way as you don't see yourself, and he is your creator.

30th day:

1. On this day you carry out concentration on the built platform. This concentration lays the basis for your work in the following month.

You should concentrate on the harmony of the World. You should see it, find it, rejoice at it, and admire it. And at the same time you wonder how the Creator could have created everything so perfectly. You admire the harmony of the World as the consequence of perfection of the Creator.

2. Seven-digit number: 1852143;
Nine-digit number: 185219351.

3. Principle based on which you build all the previous days may be the main one on this day, since in February, in the current system of chronology, 29 or 28 days, this principle on the thirtieth day gets over to the first or the second day. So, this unification shows the eternal cycle of life. Find the eternity in all your previous harmonization. Find this eternity in this simple example, since one month consists of 30 days, another, February, of 29 or 28 days and just through one month February we

have common joining of figure 30 with figure one or two. Joining of the figures various by nature and origin testifies to the unity and common nature of everyone. Find common nature in everything, in each element of information, find common nature where it is not seen at once, and find it where it is obvious, find it where it can be seen at once. And you will see, and you will become aware, and you will feel, and you will be inspired.

31st day:

1. On the thirty first day you concentrate on the separated areas of each individual volume.

Let, for example, a tree grow on a certain site of the land. You realize that there is ground below, under it. There is air above it and on each side. All these separate areas join in your consciousness by your seeing in all of them the eternal reproduction of life. The life is eternal. You have to realize it. Remember about it watching the surrounding world, feeling it, dissolving in it. Realization of this Truth will come to you: YES, THE LIFE IS ETERNAL!

2. Seven-digit number: 1532106;
Nine-digit number: 185214321.

3. You are absolutely and completely healthy and everyone around you is healthy. And the World is eternal. And all vents are creative. And always you see everything only in positive light. And everything around is favorable.

I would like to make one more remark to the given exercises. I repeat once again that you should determine yourself the number of concentrations and their duration. You have also to decide independently which result currently is the most important for you, what you should aspire to first of all.

Remember that these exercises are creative. They develop you. You will grow spiritually with the help of these concentrations, and this in its turn will help you to fulfill all these concentrations at a higher level and that will provide you bigger development and so further.

These exercises help to develop consciousness, development of events of your life in favorable direction, receiving of full value health and establishment of harmony with the pulse of the Universe.

THE WORLD TEACHER DISCLOSED
SIGNS AND EVIDENCES THAT HE'S AMONG US

CONTENT

INTRODUCTION	3
CHAPTER 1 Jeane, I found him!	5
CHAPTER 2 About Grigori Grabovoi	13
CHAPTER 3 The Grand Lama Djwhal Khul about the imminent Second Coming of the Savior in visible form.	19
CHAPTER 4 The Michel Nostradamus about the coming of the Messiah.	23
CHAPTER 5 Interesting things said by well-known Russian clairvoyant, Yuri Kretov.	27
CHAPTER 6 Grigori Rasputin - the forerunner of the arrival of the Savior?	30
CHAPTER 7 Vanga said to Grigori Grabovoi: "You are God! You will save the world!"	33
CHAPTER 8 Nol van Valer about the Second Coming of Jesus Christ.	35
CHAPTER 9 Ortodox rabbi discloses the name of the Messiah.	39
CHAPTER 10 Edgar Cayce on the "Second Coming".	43
CHAPTER 11 Grigori Grabovoi - World Teacher	45

CHAPTER 12
Nora Raimovna Morozkina about Grigori Grabovoi   **54**

CHAPTER 13
Pronouncing.   **61**

CHAPTER 14
The unexpected vision   **61**

CHAPTER 15
Ramtha about Yeshua ben Joseph.   **63**

CHAPTER 16
The false Messiahs.   **65**

CHAPTER 17
The Program Party DRUGG.   **72**

CHAPTER 18
About illegal arrest.   **74**

CHAPTER 19
About customs of prosecution.   **76**

CHAPTER 20
Interview with Susanna Dudiyeva.   **79**

CHAPTER 21
Grigori Grabovoi was released on May 21, 2010.   **86**

CHAPTER 22
Old age.   **87**

CHAPTER 23
Death is a virus in the collective consciousness of humanity.   **89**

CHAPTER 24
Speech of Andrew Poletaev, Doctor of Physical
and Mathematical Sciences, Institute of Molecular
 Biology, Moscow.   **90**

CHAPTER 25
Let's see who the Antichrist is.   **93**

CHAPTER 26
Balcan Armageddon.   **97**

CHAPTER 27
What's the main thing in the religion of Grigori Grabovoi?   **99**

CHAPTER 28
Sermon on the Religion of the World
Teacher delivered in 1999. Moscow. Russia.   **101**

CHAPTER 29
My Resume.   **110**

CHAPTER 30
Concentration exercises for every day of the month.   **110**

THE WORLD TEACHER DISCLOSED
SIGNS AND EVIDENCES THAT HE'S AMONG US

Edited by Denis Harting
Cover design : Jullian

Copyright @ 2014 by Yelena Loginova
All Right Reserved at Library of Congress USA

Printed in United State of America

ENLIGHTENMENT PUBLICATIONS

142

www.ingramcontent.com/pod-product-compliance
Lightning Source LLC
Chambersburg PA
CBHW071743150426
43191CB00010B/1672